# The Church's Healing Ministry

David Atkinson is a pastoral theologian and ethicist. A research chemist before he was ordained, he taught ethics and psychology of religion at the University of Oxford. His most recent book is *Renewing the Face of the Earth: A Theological and Pastoral Response to Climate Change* (Canterbury Press, 2008).

Prior to his retirement he was Bishop of Thetford.

Also by the same author and available
from Canterbury Press

*Renewing the Face of the Earth: A Theological and Pastoral
Response to Climate Change*

978 1 85311 898 2

'The range of topics to which David Atkinson refers, the
sources from which he draws, and the challenge of its practical
conclusions, make this book of particular interest and value.'
*Bulletin of the Society of Ordained Scientists*

# The Church's Healing Ministry

*Practical and pastoral reflections*

David Atkinson

CANTERBURY
PRESS
Norwich

© David Atkinson 2011

First published in 2011 by the Canterbury Press Norwich
Editorial office
13–17 Long Lane,
London, EC1A 9PN, UK

Canterbury Press is an imprint of Hymns Ancient and Modern Ltd
(a registered charity)
13A Hellesdon Park Road, Norwich, Norfolk, NR6 5DR, UK

www.scm-canterburypress.co.uk

Scripture quotations are from the New Revised Standard Version of
the Bible, copyright 1989 by the Division of Christian Education of
the National Council of the Churches of Christ in the USA. Used by
permission. All rights reserved.

British Library Cataloguing in Publication data

A catalogue record for this book is available
from the British Library

978 1 84825 077 2

Originated by the Manila Typesetting Company
Printed and bound in Great Britain by
CPI Antony Rowe, Chippenham, Wiltshire

# Contents

# CONTENTS

For Sue,
and for Kate and Roger,
*with gratitude*

# I

# The Church's ministry of healing

The Church's ministry of healing covers a very wide range of activities, not all compatible with one another. 'Healing Service at 6.30 p.m. Come and experience a miracle' says the poster outside a rather shabby corrugated-iron evangelical tabernacle in the inner city. People with back pain come and receive prayer. It is all very informal and rather noisy. One or two go away saying the pain has gone, others are disappointed. In the large Pentecostal church some distance away, the statement of faith includes: 'We believe that deliverance from sickness, by Divine Healing, is provided for in the Atonement.' They, too, offer services of divine healing on a regular basis. The local Reformed church, by contrast, believes that the age of miracles lasted while there were apostles, but has long since passed away, and that contemporary claims to miracles are misguided at best, and possibly of the devil. An Anglican church in the suburbs is more sedate. There is an occasional service of healing, but the context is the liturgy of the Eucharist, laying on of hands and anointing with oil, and a formal prayer.

People find it comforting to be part of a service, and some attend regularly for a sort of spiritual pick-me-up, but not many people talk about miracles. A little miracle happened, however, in one woman's lounge when a friend was praying for her, and unexpectedly she felt a significant change for the better had occurred within her body, which the doctor subsequently confirmed. So was this a 'gift of healing'?

There is the Christian doctor who believes that the restoration of God's image is spiritual and not physical, as death is inevitable, and that the priorities of the gospel are eternal salvation, not temporary respite for ailing bodies. We should not therefore, in his view, put our faith in miraculous cures. His perspective would be that we should look to the doctor for health in our bodies, and to the Church for help with our souls. On the other hand, there is the Christian health worker who wonders how Christian healing relates to the increasingly technological approach to medicine in many of our hospitals. What are we doing when we use sophisticated scanners and dialysis machines? What do we think of medical technology when we are faced with incurable conditions, and what does that do to our view of human vulnerability in the face of disease?

The health centre has a counselling agency staffed by Christians. They are seeking to express their faith through their professional work, and look with suspicion at the new Christian counselling agency that has opened in a local Methodist church hall. But what is 'Christian' counselling, and how does it relate to the accredited work of the British Association for Counselling and Psychotherapy? And what is to be made of the change of attitude among many Christians in recent years concerning such therapies as osteopathy and acupuncture? A generation ago these were suspect; now, for many people, they seem routine.

Three decades ago, a young Christian family doctor called James Casson was diagnosed with a terminal illness, and he wrote of his experiences of dying in a small booklet entitled *Dying: The Greatest Adventure of My Life*.[1] He wrote of the practical problems of dealing with cancer, he wrote of Christian hope, and he included a section on divine healing. In a measured way he argued that the medical profession should be more open to the healing love of God, but described his own 'healing' in terms of emotional strength when he was very depressed, and specific answers to prayer over some more distressing symptoms that he was sure were psychosomatic in origin:

Release came with the realization that the whole issue was out of my hands . . . the great joy was that the Lord was at the tiller,

---

1 J. Casson, *Dying: The Greatest Adventure of My Life*, Christian Medical Fellowship, 1980.

his face gently smiling and his eyes twinkling as he quietly guided me to my destination. Was I healed? Yes, I believe I was.

So it is clear that what is described as the Church's 'ministry of healing' covers a very wide range, and over the centuries it has covered most of the emphases given in the above paragraphs. It includes the Church's commitment to medical care and its own specific ministry of sacramental healing through prayer and anointing, as well as more informal approaches. The Church has been involved in the founding of hospitals: there was one founded by St Basil in the fourth century; the Augustinian canons founded St Thomas' Hospital in London in the twelfth century. St Christopher's pioneer hospice was established in Sydenham in 1967. The Church has also contributed to the training of doctors and the setting up of medical missions. In addition, the Church's pastoral ministry includes a strong interest in counselling and psychotherapy and there are a number of Christian agencies for counselling. This includes pastoral care for individuals, along with a social commitment to the health of the wider community. This is not to say, however, that the Church's role in the ministry of healing has been consistent. In different places, at different times, in different Christian denominations, the emphasis placed on healing has been very varied.

On the one hand, some parts of the Christian Church seem to have abandoned any interest in healing ministry, operating with a split view of a person that leaves healing to the medical profession while the Church concentrates on preaching the gospel for the salvation of the soul. I shall argue that this split view does not do justice to the New Testament image of people. On the other hand, parts of the Christian Church have become so absorbed with healing ministries of different sorts that they give the impression that health is a sort of commodity that can be accessed if only we say the right prayers, or do the right liturgical actions. This mechanizes health in a way that the Bible does not, and if unchecked can lead to an idolatry of health. It can also raise wholly unrealistic expectations of the miraculous healing of all disease, which can do considerable harm.

3

This book attempts to chart a course between different viewpoints, guided by the overall theme that the Church's pastoral ministry is given its meaning by, and caught up into, the ministry of Jesus. We will focus on the Church's healing ministry in its broadest sense, and the fact of pain, suffering and continuing ill health will obviously need to be part of the story. We shall discuss Christian pastoral counselling, some of the values that underlie pastoral care, and concentrate in Chapter 4 on ministry with people who are particularly vulnerable because of abuse they have suffered. We conclude by looking at the relationship between health and salvation, and explore the sacramental ministry of prayer and anointing. So our purpose is to offer some theological reflections on Christian pastoral care in relation to the question of health. For underneath all this is the question of what is meant by 'health'.

## What is health?

The word for 'good health', used in the prayer in the Third Letter of John, also means 'wholesome' and 'sound': 'Beloved, I pray that all may go well with you and that you may be in good health, just as it is well with your soul' (3 John 2). So what does 'good health' mean?

One famous, or notorious, definition of health was offered by the World Health Organization: 'Health is a state of complete physical, mental and social well-being, not simply the absence of illness and disease.' This is both too limited and too broad. It is too limited in that it makes no reference to a person's spiritual progress as part of the meaning of health, and in that it concentrates on a 'state' of well-being, whereas human life is a constantly changing journey. But it is also too broad in failing to recognize the inevitability of ageing and death, and offers too utopian a vision of life without pain, and no recognition of the redemptive possibilities that suffering can sometimes bring. More simply, and more satisfactorily, the theologian Jürgen Moltmann suggests that health is 'the strength to be human'. His conclusion is worth quoting:

If we understand health as the strength to be human, then we make being human more important than the state of being healthy. Health is not the meaning of human life. On the contrary, a person has to prove the meaning he has found in his own life in conditions of health and sickness. Only what can stand up to both health and sickness, and ultimately to living and dying, can count as a valid definition of what it means to be human.[2]

## Disease, illness and sickness

Some people understand health mostly in relation to disease: an objective condition concerned with those parts of our bodies that are not functioning properly. I visited Zambia with Christian Aid a few years ago, and met a woman, Theresa, in her late twenties, sitting on the floor of her small mud house. Her body was desperately weak through contracting the HIV virus via a blood transfusion. Her 'lack of health' was in large part due to the intrusion of a virus into her bloodstream. If health is the absence of disease, then healing becomes restoring proper functioning to an organ, or to the body as a whole. For Theresa it might have meant anti-retro-viral drugs, until something better was discovered – if she could afford them that is, and if there was nursing care available to help her take the medication.

Others understand health as the absence of illness: this is a more subjective word. When I feel ill, it may be the result of some disease, or it may come from more complicated emotional factors such as relationships being strained, or the environment in which I live being too stressful. Healing, then, comes to mean the restoration of a person's sense of their own well-being. In Theresa's case, her suffering was made considerably worse by the fact that her whole family had disowned her when she admitted to having the so-called 'stigma' of AIDS. She had been left to the care of some voluntary nurses who worked at a Catholic

---

2 J. Moltmann, *God in Creation*, SCM, 1985, p. 273.

centre on the compound where her small house was situated. They were able to call on her a few times a week, with a little food, and some oil to rub into her ulcerated skin. The obvious emotional distress of being abandoned by her family simply compounded the disease itself.

Yet others think of health primarily in relation to what we may call 'sicknesses'. We can understand this as a social definition. A person is sometimes said to be 'sick' if they do not fit in with society's understanding of what is 'normal' and 'healthy'. A few decades ago, behind the Iron Curtain, a person who did not comply with society's political ideas was defined as 'sick', and treated in a psychiatric hospital. Others are defined as 'sick' if they do not conform to what society expects of them because of their sexual orientation, or the shape of their nose, or some mental handicap; sometimes it can even be the process of simply growing old. Of course, it may be that 'society' itself is 'sick' rather than the individual who does not fit in. Either way, someone's social environment can be significant in relation both to disease and to illness.

For Theresa, her situation was made even harder by anxiety concerning her two young children. They attended a school where 75 per cent of the pupils were affected by the HIV virus within the family, and many were already orphans. When I visited the school of 730 pupils, there was a staff of ten, only two of whom were trained teachers. The sad fact was that there were several thousand unemployed teachers who had been fully trained in Zambia, but they were unemployable through lack of finance. There were insufficient resources for proper care of the children – what would ultimately happen to Theresa's? The 'sick economic context' of Theresa's society was a major factor in her own health and that of those around her.

To give a different example, down the middle of the street in Matopeni, one of the slums of Nairobi in Kenya, is an open sewer in which human waste and all other rubbish is thrown. There is a little bridge over the sewer, and people walk across this and children play and scavenge nearby. No clean water there, or toilets, or showers. The brute fact is that one in eight people on this planet has no access to clean water. Matopeni is a small settlement. Sixty per cent of the people of Nairobi live in slums. Matopeni means 'in the mud'. There is little dignity there, and health is poor. HIV and typhoid are widespread. There is lack of education, bad housing, bad food, bad clothing. So morale diminishes, behaviour becomes antisocial; men drink too much; and the young girls go into the sex industry to try to scrape together enough money to feed the children.

One local woman, Catherine Kithuku, caught a vision for change, and became determined to improve living standards. Catherine and her friend Veronica set up a community group, mostly made up of single mothers, concerned for the welfare of their children. With support from a local Christian Aid partner organization, Catherine Kithuku has been working for the Matopeni community to construct a water and sanitation block to improve health and generate a small income. This is her prayer:

I pray for change. I pray to live a clean, comfortable life, with privacy. I pray to see my family move out of slum life. I would ask people to pray for better housing, for children to be educated, for jobs for the young people, and support for single parents and the elderly. But most of all I pray for clean water. Without clean water we get sick. We have a lack of money and cannot afford to buy water. It will help bring a change in attitude. People will clean themselves more; they will clean their houses more; it will lead to a clean environment in more ways than one.[3]

'Health', then, is a broad term. It covers viruses and bacteria, and deals with the body as a functioning biological whole. It affects the individual person at many levels, physical, biological, psychological, social, moral and spiritual. Health is related to families, the individual person in a network of relationships with other people. It reaches

---

3 In January 2011, Christian Aid reported that in recent months a new drain has been constructed in the slum carrying sewage away from the settlement. Christmas 2010 was celebrated without fear of children falling ill through poor sanitation. Catherine's prayer is beginning to be answered.

out into the neighbourhood. The social setting of our lives impinges on our health in many different ways. Another dimension of health is ecological: the wider environment of clean water, traffic noise, air pollution, climate change.

The Christian ministry of healing must concern itself with all these aspects of health. From the management of disease, to nursing care; from learning through suffering to finding new ways of being strong and healthy. Christians will be interested in surgery and medication, concerned with emotional health, counselling and therapy. Christians will care about the social pressures that make for illness, and seek for justice, which is the expression of love in our social environments. Christian concern will extend to the wider environment of the planet, the air we breathe, the quality and sufficiency of food supplies, the need for clean water. Health will embrace the whole of our spiritual environment before God. We are concerned not only with removing what is wrong, but with promoting what is healthy: community care, public health, spiritual well-being.

## A whole person

Underneath these Christian concerns is the conviction that a person is not to be split up into different parts, but thought of as one spiritual–psychosomatic whole.

We recall the prayer in 3 John, where the author prays for 'good health', and then adds, 'just as it is well with your soul' (3 John 2). The impression is given that body and 'soul' are separate parts of the person. In fact, they are better understood as different perspectives on the whole person. Even the New Testament phrase 'spirit and soul and body' (1 Thess. 5.23), which looks as though it splits us up into three separate components, is used to refer to the whole person from different points of view. The nineteenth-century biblical scholar J. B. Lightfoot comments on this verse that 'spirit is the ruling faculty in man . . . through which he holds communion with the unseen world'; the soul is 'the seat of all his impulses and affections, the centre of his personality'; while the body 'links him to the material world and is the instrument of all his outward deeds'.[4] In the history of the Church there have indeed been times when Christians have operated with a split view of matter versus spirit, body versus soul, but today many are returning to the view – much more characteristic of the Bible as a whole – that human beings are complex creatures, functioning at many different levels, and in whom body and emotions, relationships and environments are all part of what it is to be human, and all these aspects have their part to play in our understanding of health. One contemporary biologist cautions against a 'reductionist' view:

If humans are to be understood essentially in terms of genes and their products, then illness is to be corrected by manipulating them. The result is drug-based medicine and genetic counseling or engineering. These can be extremely effective in certain circumstances, but medical care based on this approach focuses on illness rather than on health.[5]

## Shalom

To explore a Christian understanding of health, we need to turn to the witness of the Old and the New Testaments. We begin with one significant Hebrew word: *shalom*.

Most frequently translated 'peace', *shalom* means much more than the absence of conflict. It is also translated as good health, favour, completeness, prosperity, rest, welfare. *Shalom* carries the sense that all is well, peaceable and safe. Therefore *shalom* is much more than the absence of disease, broader even than the absence of feeling ill. Health is part of *shalom*, the wholeness of life whereby each dimension of our being – physical, relational, emotional and environmental – is open to God and God's

---

4 J. B. Lightfoot, *Notes on Epistles of St Paul*, 1895, p. 89, quoted in J. R. W. Stott, *The Message of Thessalonians*, InterVarsity Press, 1991, p. 133.

5 B. Goodwin, *How the Leopard Changed its Spots*, Princeton University Press, 2001, p. 205 (original edn 1994).

ways. The vision of peace in Isaiah 2.1–5, which could almost be a definition of *shalom*, is set in contrast to the sickness of the nation (1.5–6), its idolatry (2.6–22) and the social injustices (3.13–15) that bring the judgement that the Lord will not be a healer (3.7b).

It is a longing for *shalom* that the psalmist expresses when he writes: 'There is no soundness in my flesh because of your indignation; there is no health in my bones because of my sin' (Ps. 38.3). It is *shalom* that the psalmist celebrates: 'Let those who desire my vindication shout for joy and be glad, and say evermore, "Great is the LORD who delights in the welfare [*shalom*] of his servant", (Ps. 35.27).

The social dimension to *shalom* becomes very evident in Jeremiah's plea that the exiles should pray for the city in which they find themselves: 'But seek the welfare [*shalom*] of the city where I have sent you into exile, and pray to the LORD on its behalf, for in its welfare you will find your welfare' (Jer. 29.7).

The wider environmental dimensions of *shalom* are clear in Isaiah's vision of the coming abundance of life when all people return to the Lord and his ways:

> For you shall go out in joy, and be led back in peace; the mountains and the hills before you shall burst into song, and all the trees of the field shall clap their hands. Instead of the thorn shall come up the cypress; instead of the brier shall come up the myrtle; and it shall be to the LORD for a memorial, for an everlasting sign that shall not be cut off. (Isa. 55.12–13)

This vision speaks of a healed environment when God's kingly rule is established. As the Catholic theologian Hans Küng once famously wrote: 'God's kingdom is creation healed.'[6]

Each part of the prophecy of Isaiah has its emphasis on *shalom*. The first part of Isaiah speaks of the coming kingly rule of God's Messiah as a rule of *shalom*, of peace, justice and righteousness. The coming One is named Prince of Peace (*shalom*) (Isa. 9.6–7). In

---

6 H. Küng, *On Being a Christian*, Collins, 1977, p. 231.

the second part of Isaiah, God's kingly rule is a recapitulation of God's eternal covenant of peace: 'For the mountains may depart and the hills be removed, but my steadfast love shall not depart from you, and my covenant of peace [shalom] shall not be removed, says the LORD, who has compassion on you' (Isa. 54.10).

In the third part of Isaiah, the preacher stands in the shoes of the coming king and announces that God has anointed him 'to bring good news to the oppressed, to bind up the broken-hearted, to proclaim liberty to the captives, and release to the prisoners; to proclaim the year of the LORD's favour and the day of vengeance of our God' (Isa. 61.1–2).

Naturally, when centuries later Jesus 'went about all the cities and villages, teaching in their synagogues, and proclaiming the good news of the kingdom, and curing every disease and every sickness' (Matt. 9.35), it was understood that Jesus was the bringer of *shalom*. In fact, he applies the text from Isaiah 61 to himself in the synagogue at Nazareth (Luke 4.1–16), and Matthew records John the Baptist's question of Jesus:

'Are you the one who is to come, or are we to wait for another?' Jesus answered them, 'Go and tell John what you hear and see: the blind receive their sight, the lame walk, the lepers are cleansed, the deaf hear, the dead are raised, and the poor have good news brought to them.' (Matt. 11.3–5)

This echoes the passage in Isaiah 35.5–6, which describes God's salvation of Israel and the health-giving signs of the messianic age: salvation and health belong closely together; here is the kingdom of peace; Jesus is the bringer of *shalom*.

## Healing in the New Testament

As we will discuss more fully, Jesus exercised a very extensive ministry of healing. This ministry continues into the New Testament church, and gifts of healing were referred to in some of the New Testament epistles (1 Cor. 12.9) and the Acts of the Apostles.

The apostles demonstrated many signs and wonders among the people (Rom. 15.19; 2 Cor. 12.12), and in the post-Pentecost church many of the sick and those afflicted with unclean spirits were healed. Peter and John healed a man lame from birth, in the name of Jesus (Acts 3.6). At one time the sick were laid on cots in order that Peter's shadow might fall on them as he passed by, so that they might be healed (Acts 5.12–16). Philip was instrumental in the cure of people possessed, or suffering from paralysis (Acts 8.6–8). Paul and Barnabas were able to speak of signs and wonders (Acts 15.12), and God, we read, performed extraordinary miracles through Paul: handkerchiefs and cloths that had touched his skin were brought to the sick and they were cured (Acts 19.11–12). By prayer and the laying on of hands, Paul cured the father of Publius of his fever and dysentery (Acts 28.8).

Matthew says that disciples ministered to Christ by 'visiting those who are ill' (Matt. 25.39), and John tells us they prayed for one another 'that you may be in good health' (3 John 2). The practice of anointing with oil, and praying for those who were ill by calling for the elders of the Church, is referred to in the Letter of James (5.13–15).

Not everyone was healed, however. Paul himself refers to his own ailment as a 'thorn . . . in the flesh' (2 Cor. 12.7), with which God gave him the grace to cope. This 'thorn' has been variously interpreted as an eye disease, a form of epilepsy, a susceptibility to malaria – or maybe some psychological distress following the opposition to his ministry, or his anguish resulting from the unbelief of his Jewish compatriots. Indeed, speculation has been very wide, and certainty about this is impossible. We are told that Timothy had stomach trouble and 'frequent ailments' for which Paul prescribed 'a little wine' (1 Tim. 5.23); Epaphroditus became so ill that he nearly died (Phil. 2.27); and Paul had to leave Trophimus behind when he left Miletus, because he was ill. Weakness and illness – indeed some deaths – were put down to inappropriate use of the Lord's Supper (1 Cor. 11.30).

Jesus refers to physicians in the Gospels, even of a poor woman who had suffered at the hands of many of them (Matt. 9.12; Mark 2.17; 5.26; Luke 8.43). Luke was a doctor, described by Paul as 'the beloved physician' (Col. 4.14). Both Paul and Luke would have known the paragraphs from the second-century BC book of Sirach, which refers to medical skill, indicating that medicines are gifts of the Creator, and yet recognizing the limitations of medical intervention and the need for prayer. It even says that it can be seen as a punishment to fall into the hands of a doctor!

> Honour physicians for their services, for the Lord created them; for their gift of healing comes from the Most High, and they are rewarded by the king. The skill of physicians makes them distinguished, and in the presence of the great they are admired. The Lord created medicines out of the earth, and the sensible will not despise them. Was not water made sweet with a tree in order that its power might be known? And he gave skill to human beings that he might be glorified in his marvellous works. By them the physician heals and takes away pain; the pharmacist makes a mixture from them. God's works will never be finished; and from him health spreads over all the earth.
>
> My child, when you are ill do not delay, but pray to the Lord, and he will heal you. Give up your faults and direct your hands rightly, and cleanse your heart from all sin. Offer a sweet-smelling sacrifice, and a memorial portion of choice flour, and pour oil on your offering, as much as you can afford. Then give the physician his place, for the Lord created him; do not let him leave you, for you need him. There may come a time when recovery lies in the hands of physicians, for they too pray to the Lord that he will grant them success in diagnosis and in healing, for the sake of preserving life. He who sins against his Maker will be defiant towards the physician [or: may he fall into the hands of the physician].[7]

Because of sin and death, we need an approach to health that recognizes human frailty, suffering, disease and mortality, but we

---

7 Sirach 38.1–15.

also need one that acknowledges God's gifts of healing through medicine and pharmacy as much as through prayer.

## The healing ministry of Jesus

The pastoral ministry of the Church needs to be part of the ministry of Jesus, for he is the Church's pattern and the Church's resource. The Letter to the Ephesians makes the point that each baptized Christian is united with Christ through the Holy Spirit, and the ascended Christ sends gifts of ministry on to the members. Each has gifts of ministry to offer to the whole body of Christ (Eph. 4.1–15). When the whole body of Christ is working properly, it results in growth and upbuilds itself in love. The corporate ministry of the Christian Church, in other words, is to express and work out the ministry of the ascended Christ. Or, as we put it, Christian pastoral ministry is to be caught up into the pastoral ministry of Jesus. It is worth noting four particular aspects of Jesus' ministry of healing that are pertinent to our thinking about the Church's contemporary pastoral ministry.

First, the healing ministry of Jesus proclaims God's kingdom. When the deaf hear again, when the blind see again, when the paralysed walk again, and when the dead live again, the message is reinforced: God's kingdom brings new hope where there is despair; new life where there is death, a renewal of health and well-being.

Again and again, Jesus breaks the rules. He touches a leper, even though leprosy made a person unclean. He touches the woman who has a discharge of blood, even though that was thought to be ritually unclean. He reaches out to the dead body of the son of the widow of Nain, even though touching the dead makes one unclean. God's kingly rule in Jesus breaks down barriers of exclusion that prevent people hearing God's welcome. It places the law in the richer, healing context of grace.

If the pastoral ministry of the Christian Church is to be caught up into the ministry of Jesus, it needs to be understood as part of the gracious work of God's kingdom, bringing life to individuals, breaking down the barriers that stop people hearing God's welcome.

Second, the healings of Jesus were community events. Usually they were in public – visible signs of God's kingdom. When Bartimaeus is healed of his blindness,[8] Jesus faces him with his own responsibility and needs by asking: 'What do you want me to do for you?' Jesus hands responsibility and choice back to Bartimaeus. But everyone who is watching is confronted with the presence of God's kingdom power – what does this mean for them? Is Jesus, perhaps, confronting the whole community with its blindness and responsibility and choice? In such healing events, society as a whole is called to the bar of God's kingly rule.

A further social dimension to the healings of Jesus can be seen in his attitude to the demonic. As Jeffrey John makes clear, the New Testament uses the same terms 'principalities and powers' to refer both to supernatural forces, and also to 'the very real powers – armies, nations, institutions, individuals – which represent them on earth . . . The freedom Jesus brings is freedom from both personal and systemic evil; his confrontation with the demons parallels and symbolizes his confrontation with the Jewish authorities. The relevance of this for us is that 'the healing Jesus brings is as necessary for systems and societies as it is for individuals'.[9]

The pastoral ministry of the Christian Church, then, needs to be concerned not only with the individual, but with the whole society in which that person's life story is set, and this takes us into political questions of community health, as well as questions of deliverance from 'principalities and powers'.

Third, the healing ministry of Jesus changed people's priorities. This is nicely illustrated in the story of Zacchaeus – the chief tax collector who had been economical with the truth.[10] After his encounter with Jesus, Zacchaeus promised to return goods to people whom he had defrauded, and his business priorities are

8 Mark 10.46–52.

9 J. John, *The Meaning in the Miracles*, Canterbury Press, 2001, pp. 14, 15.

10 Luke 19.2–10.

turned around in the light of God's rule. And Jesus said to him, 'Today salvation has come to this house.' Or, as William Tyndale's translation has it, 'Today, health has come to this house.'

If the pastoral ministry of the Christian Church is to be caught up into the ministry of Jesus, it needs to be concerned with life-style as well as with cure, with ethics as well as with feelings, with business as well as with private life. God's kingly rule concerns all of life at all levels – as must the Church's ministry.

Fourth, healing is linked to forgiveness. Four friends bring a paralysed man to Jesus and, because of the crowds, let him down through a hole in the ceiling.[11] Jesus first says, 'Your sins are forgiven.' Then later says, 'Take up your bed and walk.' The healing work of Jesus touches this person's need for forgiveness as well as his hope to walk again.

Healing at all levels comes from God. This is beautifully expressed in the words of the prayer after communion in *The Book of Common Prayer*, which thanks God for 'the forgiveness of our sins, and all other benefits of his passion'. Those 'other benefits' we can take to include the ministry of healing and wider pastoral care.

God, it seems, sometimes withholds healing at one level in order to heal us in other ways first. Sometimes we need to hear about the forgiveness of our sins before we can receive the other word about health for our bodies. Healing is a process: it doesn't happen all at once. The theologian T. F. Torrance referred to 'eschatological reserve', by which I think he meant there is a gap between the word of forgiveness and the word of full healing. With this paralysed man, the gap was a few minutes; with some of us it takes a lifetime.

In the cross of Jesus, the word of forgiveness has been spoken, and in that sense there is healing in the cross: 'By his wounds you have been healed.'[12] But the working out of that promise takes a life of growing into wholeness. God's word of health comes to us sometimes just in part in this life, and in its fullness not until

---

11 Mark 2.4–12.
12 Isa. 53.5.

we reach the fullness of the kingdom. The Church's ministry of healing – and indeed all our pastoral ministry – takes place in that gap between the presence of God's kingdom in the life and death and resurrection of Jesus – with all the blessings that flow to us from that here and now – and the fullness of that kingdom in the life to come.

And it is that kingdom that is inaugurated in the resurrection of Jesus from the dead. The resurrection demonstrates the messianic hope that Jesus is the Messiah who brings *shalom*. It is an affirmation of creation and the beginning of its healing.

The resurrection is the resurrection of the body, which gives to our bodily life a value and meaning to be cherished. It established the victory of the cross, and provides the hope that one day there will be no more death, nor crying, nor pain. And it is the resurrection of Jesus that gives power to the Church's pastoral ministry: the Church lives in the power of the Spirit given through the resurrection of Jesus.

## Historical sketch

After New Testament times, there considerable evidence for a continuing charismatic healing ministry being exercised by the early Christian Church, and there are records of healing miracles during the first three centuries of the Church's life.[13] There seem to have been close links between the Church and medical practice, but over time the Church's healing ministry became more sacramental, combined with anointing and exorcisms. During the Middle Ages, around the eleventh and twelfth centuries, with the growth of monastic orders, there is a phase of records of miraculous healings, often through contact with the relics of saints. Despite caution from some church leaders, at the level of popular devotion much of the healing ministry of the Church was associated with magic at this time.

---

13 E. Frost, *Christian Healing*, Mowbray, 1940; G. R. Evans, ed., *A History of Pastoral Care*, Cassell, 2000.

By the sixteenth century, at the time of the Reformation, many Christians attempted to take the magic out of religion.[14] Many believed that illness was sent by God, and that suffering was to be endured patiently. Neither of the great continental Reformers, Luther or Calvin, believed in miraculous physical healings, but concentrated on the miracle of the spiritual healing of the soul. The first Anglican prayer book of Thomas Cranmer, in 1549, provided an 'Order for the Visitation of the Sick', which included a long exhortation reminding the ill person that sickness is 'God's Visitation', and that they should 'take in good worthe the chastisement of the Lord: for whom the Lord loveth he chastiseth'. It concluded with a form of anointing with oil – anointing that was omitted from Cranmer's second prayer book of 1552.

Since the Reformation, the split between Church and medical practice, fed by a dualistic view of human nature separating body from soul, has developed still further. During the seventeenth century, with the growth of the view of the world as a large machine, working according to Newton's laws, there emerged a large split in some people's minds between the physical world, which they believed could be understood by science and medicine, and the spiritual world, which was of concern to God. Medicine and religion tended to be kept in separate compartments. People went to the priest to confess their sins, and to the doctor for their physical health. More recently, and in the twentieth century in particular, with the founding of various Guilds of Health, the Church's healing ministry has become more identified with the sacramental ministry, and the Church's ministry of healing has become well established, clergy working alongside medical professionals in striving for the health of the 'whole person'. In particular, the growth of the Pentecostal churches in the twentieth century, and of the charismatic movement within older Christian denominations, has brought 'gifts of healing' within the Church to greater prominence. In addition, the development of social and political dimensions to health

---

14 K. Thomas, *Religion and the Decline of Magic*, Weidenfeld & Nicolson, 1971, Penguin, 1973.

within communities has been explored from a Christian perspective and implications drawn for the corporate and social aspects of the Church's ministry to the sick.

## Pastoral care today

If we understand the Church's pastoral ministry in relation to questions of health to include the three aspects of 'shepherding' identified by Hiltner[15] (healing, sustaining and guiding), as well as co-operation with the medical profession, involvement in counselling and psychotherapy for those with emotional problems, the ministry of deliverance in relation to 'principalities and powers', and the social dimensions of community health, we can see that there is a considerable variety of Christian responses to questions of sickness and health. Each in their different ways can express something of the healing ministry of Jesus; each can proclaim God's kingdom of *shalom*.

We can identify a number of primary models of Christian pastoral care in the Church today, each of which can relate to the ministry of healing:

### *Proclamation and teaching model*

For some Christians, the primary task of Christian ministry is the proclamation of the gospel, often identified as expository preaching, teaching, and verbal evangelism. Certainly all the thousands who listened to Dr Lloyd-Jones preach in the 1960s at Westminster Chapel heard sermons that brought the text of Scripture in touch with people's personal needs, and the word of God struck home in a life-changing and often healing way. There can be a very powerful pastoral theology of preaching, but there is also a danger of making this model the sum total of pastoral care. The preacher can hide defensively behind the

---

15 S. Hiltner, *Preface to Pastoral Theology*, Abingdon Press, 1958.

expository mode, and preaching can become cerebral and didactic in a way that fails to meet people 'where they are'. In the book of Job, Eliphaz, Bildad and Zophar in their different ways were no doubt excellent expositors, but they did not help to meet Job's need: 'Miserable comforters are you all!'[16]

## Nurture model

Some patterns of discipleship – ranging from Wesley's class meetings, to Christian summer camps – provide a Christian approach whereby young people in particular are nurtured and cared for by older like-minded Christians (a model that seems so attractive that the atheist camps supported by Richard Dawkins have taken it over). Fellowship groups, Bible studies, home groups and cell churches can all provide a context not only for worship and service, but for mutual support – sometimes even mutual therapy. This avoids the guru-mentality of the preaching model, but in some churches hierarchies of 'shepherding' and authority structures are developed that are not always liberating. There are variants on this model in the sort of support groups set up for survivors of abuse and, in a different way, groups aiming to enable sex offenders to be accountable when they return to the community.

## Service model

By 'service' I mean pastoral ministry that is motivated by compassion and emphasizes the importance of social welfare, and also the political commitment to social justice concerning the environments in which people live. Many church groups and church institutions are involved in community health projects, as advocates for justice in health-care delivery and the social changes that promote healthy living.

---

16 Job 16.2.

There are organizations such as Welcare in Southwark Diocese, which 'offers services to families to help improve the quality of their lives, and enables them to fulfil their potential'. There are working groups trying to implement the recommendations of *Time for Action*, the CTBI Report on survivors of abuse. There are also various global organizations ranging from Christian Aid to Jubilee 2000, which act politically against poverty out of the conviction that each person bears God's image and has a right to certain basic necessities.

A further dimension to the service model is the Church's concern with what has come to be called 'community health'. This moves concern for health beyond a narrowly medical model, and recognizes dimensions to health that are more public and social. It is concerned with issues relating to the environment, to air pollution, to the availability of clean water, to matters concerning transport. Behind such concerns lies the Christian conviction that there needs to be equality of opportunity for access to the rich resources of God's world, and an equitable distribution of the things that contribute towards good health. Alongside the Christian concern for individual health, therefore, some churches – inspired by the calling to live out the justice of God in all human affairs – develop local community links for the sharing of resources, are open to the needs of the wider world (particularly those parts that are the most poor and disadvantaged), and seek to contribute to policy-making at community level. Often the Church contributes to debates about education – clearly a key factor in the promotion of good community health – and the promotion of a healthy lifestyle.[17]

## Therapy model

There is significant Christian involvement in the worlds of counselling and psychotherapy, and this has been well documented

---

17 cf. T. Drummond, 'Healing Words: Health and the Church', in M. Simmons, ed., *Street Credo*, Lemos & Crane, 1999.

by Roger Hurding in *Roots and Shoots*.[18] Counselling merges into prayer for inner healing in writers such as David Seamands, Ruth Carter-Stapleton and Francis MacNutt. There was a huge impetus to the counselling dimension of pastoral care some years ago, stimulated by the work of Frank Lake in *Clinical Theology*, and by the development of numerous so-called 'Christian counselling' agencies. Some such groups sought to marry biblical theology and the insights of the secular human sciences. At one extreme, 'Christian counselling' was defined in terms of biblical parameters only, and a narrow form of counselling – almost akin to preaching – developed. Many felt that this stance showed too little sensitivity to human frailty and hurt, too little attention to God's gracious presence, too little awareness of the Spirit of God at work in secular psychologies – and too much emphasis on human responsibility for change, and an inappropriate use of the Bible. At the other end of the spectrum, 'Counselling in a Christian context' was largely indistinguishable from many other human relations-based models, though developed with Christian perspectives and Christian motivation. To reduce all pastoral care to counselling, however, suggests that all pastoral care is problem-centred, whereas its concerns are the whole of a person's life journey within the family and the community. It tends to be too individualistic, whereas the Christian life is essentially corporate and social. There have been some attempts to link pastoral counselling to the work of spiritual direction.

## Charismatic/Pentecostal model

The renewed interest in the Gifts of the Spirit in the Pentecostal denominations during the twentieth century, and in the charismatic renewal from the 1960s onwards in many 'mainline' denominations, led to a growth in the ministry of healing from a 'charismatic' perspective. This has tended to be informal, and sometimes disorderly, and has received notoriety in some

---

18 Hodder & Stoughton, 1986.

examples of American TV evangelism. The theological conviction behind this approach is that Jesus heals today just as he did when he walked the earth, and that the full gospel includes physical healing as well as spiritual salvation. There are certainly examples of what could be called miraculous changes in people (as we shall discuss later), but the theological basis for this is not straightforward. Yet the raising of expectations that everyone will be healed of all disease cannot be squared with the continuing illness that the New Testament itself documents.

## Sacramental model

Many churches offer a 'service of prayer for healing', which is typically in the context of the Eucharist. Sometimes this involves prayer for healing, with anointing with oil, and laying on of hands, using a formal liturgy. Sometimes an offer is made of 'someone to pray with you' after a person has received communion, and the context then is likely to be more informal and less liturgical. For some churches this is a regular part of weekly ministry; for others there is a special occasion, say once a month, when a Healing Eucharist is held.

One particular dimension of sacramental ministry was developed by Dr Kenneth McAll, and documented in his book, *Healing the Family Tree*.[19] McAll's insight was that sometimes a person's psychological disturbance may be due to a disturbed family history, and that prayer should be not only for the suffering person in the present, but also for ancestors. His preferred 'medicine' was a special Eucharist in which both the person, and the family tree, was offered to God in the context of prayer, and healing sought for both.

Some of these models will form the basis for further discussion in the following chapters. But we begin with that hardest of all subjects for people of faith – the fact that God allows pain and suffering at all – and examine the possibilities of seeing suffering

---

19  K. McAll, *Healing the Family Tree*, Sheldon Press, 1982.

creatively and positively as part of the meaning of growing into health. We shall then look at aspects of the counselling ministry of the Church, and some of the values underlying all pastoral ministry, using the experience of survivors of abuse as examples for our exploration of justice and forgiveness. And we shall return to the sacramental model of healing, to root the various aspects of health within the liturgical life of the Church. Our overall aim is to discuss further what it means to be caught up into the healing ministry of Jesus, and for the Church to be an agent of God's kingdom of *shalom*.

# 2

# The pain that heals

'How can you believe in a God of love who allows this?' The question is asked by colleagues in the school staff room, by neighbours over the fence. It is asked at the bedside of the young girl dying of cancer, and by the partner of the young man dying of motor neurone disease. It was asked at the Lisbon earthquake in 1755 when tens of thousands of people died. It was asked at Aberfan in 1966 when 144 people (115 of them children) lost their lives as a mountain of coal waste collapsed on the village. It was on the lips of many watching television news of the Boxing Day south-Asia tsunami of 2004 or the Pakistan floods.

There is no pastoral ministry that does not come up against the difficult problem of innocent human suffering, and apparently pointless pain. There is no healing ministry that can avoid the question of the absence of healing, the fact that there are some situations and some people that seemingly cannot be healed, the ever-present fact of disease and ill-health, the inevitability of age-ing and death. The existence of suffering in the world poses one of the hardest questions of all to people of faith. Why does a good God allow such suffering? Why does God apparently do little to alleviate it?

In Chapter 1, I referred to a life of 'growing into wholeness', and the sort of pastoral ministry that can help others in that process – growing into God's *shalom*, made available to us in Jesus. And we all know that there are times when growing is pain-ful, and we talk about 'growing pains'. But some of the unexplained pain that some people suffer seems to be in a different league. In this chapter we cannot address all the questions of theodicy, about which long books have been written,[1] but we do try to explore some of the painful aspects of growing into wholeness – what the pathologist and Anglican priest Martin Israel in his book of the same title calls 'The Pain that Heals'. One helpful way into some of these aspects is the remarkable poem in the Bible that we call the Book of Job,[2] which raises these questions in a particularly poignant way.

## The story of Job

Job is a man who suffers intolerably, and seemingly endlessly, and when we read his story we find ourselves caught up in his pain, and the injustice of it all. He envelopes us in his plea to God to tell him what on earth is going on. He loses his family, his home, his servants, his flocks and cattle, his health, his stability, his friendship with his wife, his sense of God's presence. He is abandoned by everyone. There is nothing anyone can say that can bring any comfort. And yet he is a good man, a godly man, a man who believed that God is just:

> Why is light given to one who cannot see the way, whom God has fenced in? For my sighing comes like my bread, and my groanings are poured out like water. Truly the thing that I fear comes upon me, and what I dread befalls me. I am not at ease, nor am I quiet; I have no rest; but trouble comes.[3]

For most of the book, the hand of God is hidden. We, the readers, are told that there is more to this than meets the eye, and we are let into some of the secrets of the heavenly court in the first chapter of the book. We are given hints that, alongside the story of Job, another story is being told – a story in which God is

---

1 For example, J. Hick, *Evil and the God of Love*, Macmillan, 1966; P. Vardy, *The Puzzle of Evil*, HarperCollins, 1992; N. T. Wright, *Evil and the Justice of God*, SPCK, 2006.

2 Cf. my fuller study in *The Message of Job*, InterVarsity Press, 1991.

3 Job 3.23–26.

firmly in control. But Job does not see this. To him, God has let him down. Job sees only the tangled threads, which mean nothing. He cannot see the other side of the tapestry where a picture begins to make some sense.

And Job's faith is no answer to his predicament; in fact, it makes it worse. The most difficult part of the story of Job is not only the physical and emotional suffering of an innocent person, but that everything Job had believed about God is called into question, leaving him only with the agonized cry, 'My God, why?'

Why did I not die at birth?[4] Why do you hide your face, and count me as your enemy?[5] Why do the wicked live on, reach old age, and grow mighty in power?[6]

It is precisely because Job is a believer in God's goodness that suffering is such a moral, theological and spiritual problem. Otherwise, I suppose, it would just be 'one of those things'. In *River out of Eden*, the atheist Richard Dawkins makes this melancholy judgement: 'The universe we observe has precisely the properties we should expect if there is, at bottom, no design, no purpose, no evil and no good, nothing but blind, pitiless indifference'. The French biologist Jacques Monod had said much the same years earlier: 'The ancient covenant is in pieces; man at last knows that he is alone in the unfeeling immensity of the universe, out of which he emerged only by chance.'[7] But Job *did* believe in the ancient covenant: that was his problem. He *did* think there was design and purpose, evil and good, and he could not understand why the God of the covenant was seemingly allowing him to experience so much that was evil, when he knew himself to be good.

There is some resonance in Job with C. S. Lewis's struggle after the death of his wife, which he records in his book, *A Grief Observed*. At one painful point, he even calls God the 'Cosmic

---

4 Job 3.11.

5 Job 13.24.

6 Job 21.7.

7 R. J. Dawkins, *River out of Eden*, Basic Books, 1995, p. 133; Monod, *Chance and Necessity*, Alfred A. Knopf, 1971, p. 167.

Sadist': 'Talk to me about the truth of religion, and I'll listen gladly; talk to me about the duty of religion and I'll listen submissively. But don't come talking to me about the consolations of religion, or I shall suspect that you don't understand.'[8]

As the book of Job unfolds, we are given a picture of Job in the depths of despair, and we are treated to the spectacle of three of Job's friends offering what is meant to be comforting advice. All of them make things worse – though that is not quite fair to the whole picture we are given of them. The first thing we hear of these friends is that they come and sit silently with Job on the ground for seven days and seven nights. They were able to offer him the consolation of silent presence, which was perhaps, at that stage of his journey, exactly what Job needed. But this did not last. Soon Job's silence gives way to lament, and we can chart his movement from a period of numbness to anger, through disbelief to despair, and eventually to defiance. What we now call the stages of grieving or bereavement are all experienced by Job.

In tracing Job's journey of faith and suffering, we encounter what we may call his anger at the arrows of God (6–7); his despair before the mightiness of God (9–10); his terror at God's absence and at God's presence (12–14). There is a time when hope of vindication begins to grow (16–17), and he proclaims that his Redeemer lives! (19). But Job complains about God's ways (21); expresses a longing for communion with God (23–24), and makes his last defiant stand against God (29–31).

Throughout, we are caught up into the pain and perplexity of Job's outrage at what he perceives to be the silence of God's presence – even the silence of God's absence. Why has God let him down?

## Job's three friends

In several cycles of speeches, Job's three friends try to argue with him. Eliphaz begins by recognizing that Job is a good man, reminding him

---

8  C. S. Lewis, *A Grief Observed*, Faber & Faber, 1961, p. 23.

that we live in a moral universe: that you reap what you sow. But then he approaches Job on the basis of a logic that argues: everything you reap must come from something you have sown. In other words, Job, because you are reaping disaster, you must have sown wrongdoing. Eliphaz offers a cold logic, which is very far from the response of a living faith in a living God. It is the Eliphaz mistake that lies behind much of the so-called 'prosperity theology': that doing good will bring health and prosperity, with the corollary drawn that if you are suffering it must be because of your sins. Although, of course, a sinful lifestyle sometimes leads directly to ill health, and a good lifestyle is important in promoting health, that is very different from saying that one person's illness must necessarily be the result of their sins. In the New Testament, Jesus knocks this Eliphaz mistake very clearly on the head. 'Rabbi, who sinned, this man or his parents, that he was born blind?' the disciples asked Jesus in John 9.2. Jesus does not accept the question in those terms. It was not that this man or his parents had sinned, he replied, but that the works of God might be revealed in the man. Those 18 who were killed when the tower of Siloam fell on them, Jesus asks, were they worse offenders than all the others living in Jerusalem (Luke 13.4)? No: all are equally called to repentance (Luke 13.5).

Bildad is Job's second interlocutor. He is the old traditionalist, quoting theology, and talking a lot about God's justice. Buck up, Job, he seems to say, God cannot really be letting you down; everything is going to be all right. The Bildad mistake is too small and too static a view of God. He has no place for God's surprise.

Friend number three is Zophar, not a pleasant person; an intellectual prig. As one commentator said of him: 'he never lets facts interfere with his theories'. He is full of his own importance and never engages with Job's suffering at all. Zophar unfortunately knows all the answers.

All three friends do their best, but they all miss Job's need. Eliphaz talks about God's transcendence and holiness; Bildad speaks about God's power and justice; Zophar talks of God's inscrutable wisdom. They are all latching on to part of the truth. Together they seem to put together the classic philosophical arguments against a good God allowing evil, but none of them can reach Job in his pain.

Interspersed with these speeches are replies from Job, which can be summarized rather generally, if rather too politely, as 'a fat lot of use you are'.

## Two interludes

And then after 27 chapters of unrelieved tension and anguish, something strange happens in the poem. There are two interludes in which we the readers are given a breathing space from all this trauma.

The first interlude is Job 28, altogether different from everything else we have read. It is a wonderful reflection on wisdom. True wisdom, we discover, is not just logic, or simply tradition, or intellectual cleverness such as we have seen in the three counsellors. True wisdom is the gift of the living God who makes himself known in unexpected ways. The image used in Job 28 is of mining, of digging into the depths and discovering precious things. There are sometimes jewels to be found in the darkness.

And then there is another interlude in the poem as we have it in our Bibles. Elihu walks on to the stage. He is a young man, in some ways more like a clown than a counsellor. He says a lot, not much of it very different from the other three friends. But every now and then there is a new shaft of light, a jewel glistening in the darkness. The most important thing Elihu achieves is to face Job with the possibility that God may be doing something very positive, even though Job could only feel the negative: 'God indeed does all these things, twice, three times, with mortals, to bring back their souls from the Pit, so that they may see the light of life.'[9]

He puts it to Job: could God be using your suffering creatively?

Creative suffering? It is hard to express this in the right words. Put it one way and it sounds as though God inflicts pain on

---

9 Job 33. 29–30.

his children for their good – in other words, could he, after all, be the Cosmic Sadist that C. S. Lewis speaks of? That is surely misleading. Elihu puts it better. Paul Tournier, the Swiss doctor, quoting a Dr Haynal, puts it another way. Tournier asks about the relationship that exists between suffering and creativity . . . not a relationship of cause and effect.

> Rather the person matures, develops, becomes more creative, not because of the deprivation in itself, but through his own active response to misfortune, through the struggle to come to terms with it, and . . . overcome it, even if, in spite of everything, there is no cure.[10]

Elihu does not quite get that far, but he gives hints about what Frances Young calls the 'wildness' in God's ordering of things – or of what Mr Beaver in *The Lion, the Witch and the Wardrobe* says of Aslan:

> He'll be coming and going. One day you'll see him and another you won't. He doesn't like being tied down . . . It is quite all right, he'll often drop in. Only you mustn't press him. He's wild you know. Not like a tame lion.[11]

Of course, at the end of the story of Job, God himself does break the silence. He speaks to Job out of the whirlwind. It is a most unexpected speech, not answering Job's questions at all. But what God's word does is show to Job that this is God's world, that there is another story of which Job's story is just a part, and that in his inscrutable providence, God has – despite all appearances – never let go of his hand.

In the Lord's speech from the whirlwind (38–42), God indicates the divine wisdom, seen throughout the whole of the rest of creation (38–39); he illustrates his supreme power over even the

---

10 P. Tournier, *Creative Suffering*, SCM, 1982, p. 28.
11 C. S. Lewis, *The Lion, the Witch and the Wardrobe*, Fontana, 1980, p. 168 (original edn 1950).

great monsters that cause such fear, the hippo and the crocodile (40); and demonstrates his justice (40.6–14). He begins with this poignant question to Job:

> 'Where were you when I laid the foundation of the earth? Tell me, if you have understanding. Who determined its measurements – surely you know! Or who stretched the line upon it? On what were its bases sunk, or who laid its cornerstone when the morning stars sang together and all the heavenly beings shouted for joy?'[12]

That insight was hinted at earlier in the most significant thing that Elihu had said: 'He delivers the afflicted by their affliction, and opens their ear by adversity' (36.15). Elihu moves from a backward-looking retributive understanding of suffering, such as we have found in the other three friends, to a forward-looking redemptive and healing one. Job has not been abandoned. His whole series of the most awful experiences are part of a process through which ultimately there is healing. In his book, *The Pain that Heals,* Martin Israel writes: 'It is one of the fundamental contributions of pain to make people wake up to a deeper quality of existence and to seek evidence for meaning in their lives beyond the immediate sensations that arrest their attention.'[13]

Simone Weil comments that the extreme greatness of Christianity lies in the fact that it does not seek a supernatural remedy for suffering, but a supernatural use for it.


## Is there a suffering that heals?

The fullest answer to that question needs to be based on the fact that we now read the story of Job from the perspective of the New Testament, through a window framed by the cross. The suffering and death of Jesus is not given to us as an argument

---

12 Job 38.4–7.
13 M. Israel, *The Pain that Heals,* Hodder & Stoughton, 1981, p. 12.

about logic; it is not presented primarily as a demonstration of God's power; it is not even discussed in the first instance in terms of justice – though all of these factors have their part to play. The suffering of Jesus is the suffering of God. Not the distant God of Eliphaz, Bildad and Zophar who cannot touch Job in his pain, but the suffering of a God who comes where we are, takes our sufferings on to his shoulders, shares our abandonment, dies our death. Jesus takes Job's cry on to his own lips: 'My God, why?'

And that becomes the basis for the confidence the apostle Paul finds in his own unexplained suffering and struggle: 'My grace is sufficient for you; for power is made perfect in weakness' (2 Cor. 12.9).

Nicholas Wolterstorff, American professor of philosophy, wrote this poignant paragraph in his little book, *Lament for a Son*. Some years ago, his 25-year-old son was killed in a climbing accident in Austria. Wolterstorff wrote:

> For a long time I knew that God is not the impassive, unresponsive, unchanging being portrayed by the classical theologians. I knew of the pathos of God. I knew of God's response of delight and his response of displeasure. But strangely, his suffering I never saw before . . . Through the prism of my tears I have seen a suffering God . . . God is love, that is why he suffers. To love our suffering world is to suffer. God so suffered for the world that he gave up his only Son to suffering. The one who does not see God's suffering does not see his love. God is suffering love. So suffering is down at the centre of things, deep down where the meaning is. Suffering is the meaning of our world. For Love is the meaning. And Love suffers. The tears of God are the meaning of history.[14]

A perspective such as the book of Job will be needed in the light of natural disasters that confront us with the question of God's purposes in creation in the face of innocent suffering. As we have

---

14 N. Wolterstorff, *Lament for a Son*, Eerdmans, 1987, pp. 81 and 90.

seen, it is a book not only about the puzzle of suffering, but also about the puzzle of persistent hope in spite of appearances, and of a faith that God can bring a greater good even out of the most devastating pain. In God's speech, Job is brought face to face with what we would call 'natural evils' – including the tempests and earthquakes that seem to be the responsibility of the Creator. Struggling towards an answer to this most difficult of questions, John Polkinghorne, distinguished physicist and ordained priest, develops what he calls a 'free-process defence':

> In his great act of creation I believe that God allows the physical world to be itself, not in Manichaean opposition to him, but in that independence which is Love's gift of freedom to the one beloved. The world is endowed in its fundamental constitution with an anthropic potentiality which makes it capable of fruitful evolution. The exploration and realization of that potentiality is achieved by the universe through the continual interplay of chance and necessity within its unfolding process.[15]

The tsunami of Boxing Day 2004, then, was not a vindictive God punishing innocent people. It was the outworking of the physical processes of shifting tectonic plates that is part of the freedom God has given the world to be itself – a freedom that has 'anthropic potentiality' to enable the universe to be capable of being our home, and not only ours, but the home of all living things, a multitude of species of animals and plants that, as Job was to learn, God has provided for. Such a defence must not, however, be read as resignation in the face of suffering. On the contrary, it must rouse us to compassion and to action.

When we try to cope with innocent suffering and apparently needless and pointless pain in our fellow human beings, we do not do so by simply accepting what is, but rather with the conviction, so well put by the former Archbishop of Canterbury, Donald Coggan: 'Jesus, when faced with suffering in others, invariably shows himself to be a fighter.' A number of times in

---

15  J. Polkinghorne, *Science and Providence*, SPCK, 1989, p. 66.

the Gospels, Jesus is described as being 'moved with compassion towards' (that is, suffering with) people who are suffering. His healing ministry was the outworking of his compassion. His was not a fatalistic acceptance of suffering as, it seems, we find in Richard Dawkins, who suggests that it is just one of those things. In Jesus' case there was both an acknowledgement of the reality of pain and suffering in the world, and a compassionate fight against disease, illness, sickness and pain. Nowhere is his attitude more starkly put than in the narrative of the death of Lazarus in John 11. At the grave of his friend, we read that Jesus was 'greatly disturbed in spirit and deeply moved' (John 11.33). The language is that of 'groaning in the spirit', even 'snorting'. Jesus is angered by the intrusion of death into God's world, and he confronts it by calling Lazarus forth from the grave. The American thinker Francis Schaeffer comments on the dilemma in Albert Camus's book, *The Plague*, in which the choice is to side with the doctor against God by fighting the plague, or join with the priest on God's side, and be much less than human by not fighting the plague. Schaeffer argues that Jesus, standing at the tomb of Lazarus, makes it clear that the Christian is not faced with such a choice: 'A Christian can fight with compassion what is wrong in the world, and know that as he hates these things, God hates them too. God hates them to the high price of the death of Christ.'[16]

God give us grace in our sufferings, and as in pastoral ministry we contemplate the sufferings of others and of the world, the grace to be filled with the compassion of Christ. May we see through our tears the tears of God, and by them be transformed.

---

16 F. Schaeffer, *The God Who Is There*, Hodder & Stoughton, 1968, p. 107.

# 3

# Emotional health:
# Christians and counselling

The Oxford Christian Institute for Counselling (OCIC) was born in 1985, when a group of us – including a therapist, a GP, a social worker, and others – became aware that the full range of personal, emotional, psychological and spiritual needs of people we knew were not being catered for by the pastoral ministry of some local churches. It seemed they were also not being helped by the statutory psychotherapy services which, so it was thought, took little interest in a person's spiritual life. In addition, there were a number of Christians who did not wish to trust themselves to the 'secular' counselling world. Would there be mileage, we wondered, in setting up a counselling service in a Christian context? After wide consultation with church leaders and some professionals in the medical, psychiatric, psychotherapeutic and social services contexts, OCIC was founded as a charitable trust and a company limited by guarantee. As I write, OCIC has just celebrated its 25th birthday, and is still meeting a need.

The objectives for which the Institute was established were described in its Memorandum of Association:

To advance the Christian religion by:

(a) providing a counselling service in a Christian context to people in appropriate need in Oxford and the surrounding districts;
(b) providing support and supervision for those involved in counselling on behalf of the Institute; and

(c) providing educational, training and study facilities for those Christians involved in counselling on behalf of the Institute.

The relationship with local churches, though, turned out to be somewhat ambiguous, so much so that I wrote in the 1992 Newsletter:

> The Christian Church from its very beginnings has been offering a ministry of caring and counselling as part of its life as a worshipping, sacramental community of members of the Body of Christ. In the last few decades, partly through the secularization in society, partly through the rise of new therapies, partly through the Church losing its nerve, 'counselling' has grown rapidly in the secular world. OCIC and other Christian counselling organizations have been seeking to bring some of the resources, skills and insights of the 'helping professions' and the therapies into the service of Christ and the Gospel. We have sought to provide a service which complements and supports the caring and counselling work of local churches.

The danger of groups like OCIC, though, is that the impression can be created that counselling and caring in a Christian context only happen there. But such groups are outside the regular worshipping, praying, sacramental community where the pastoral caring and counselling ministry really belongs. As Christian people in churches we need to recover our nerve, and learn how to care for one another again. My article continued:

> We can all help one another to be better carers, better listeners. If OCIC were really to succeed in helping local churches to provide such therapeutic relationships, as an expression of the Gospel of Christ, then – at least in this respect – OCIC would not need to exist.

## 'Christian counselling'?

Not everyone, of course, was persuaded that setting up OCIC was a good idea. One local priest said, 'Christian counselling is a contradiction in terms. There is no such thing as Christian engineering, or Christian mathematics. Counselling is counselling is counselling – it just muddies the waters to speak of "Christian" counselling as though it were something distinctive.'

In fact, OCIC had very deliberately described itself as providing 'Counselling in a Christian context', being very aware that there are some groups who *do* speak of 'Christian counselling'. Sometimes this indicates that there is a particular sort of technique such as 'confrontation with the text of Scripture', as in the writings of the American Reformed Christian Jay Adams,[1] or as in 'prayer counselling', which at its worst can degenerate into a grossly unacceptable manipulative technique in which the counsellor says things to God that he or she has not said to the client. However, as I shall argue, I do believe there is something distinctive about the context – particularly the context of assumed values – in which counselling is offered, and would wish to defend OCIC's 'counselling in a Christian context' as an appropriate approach. Christian faith, I argue, has very particular contributions to make to the understanding and practice of counselling work. I believe that the pastoral ministry of the Christian Church needs to learn from the helping professions, but also that the helping professions can benefit from some of the theological insights of the Christian Church.

## Fully alive

The New Testament word often translated as the verb 'counsel' is *parakaleo*, and the noun is *paraklesis*. Its root meaning is 'call alongside', which is not too far from our contemporary concepts of empathy, warmth and respect. However, we find it used in the New Testament with a range of meanings from fairly directive to fairly non-directive responses to human need. 'Counselling' in New Testament terms is a broad concept, and what we now recognize as professional counselling is just a part of this. It includes encouragement, exhortation and appeal as well as comfort and

---

1 For example, *Competent to Counsel*, Baker Book House, 1970.

consolation. It probably covers the whole range of what today we recognize as a spectrum from the ministries of pastoral care, through pastoral counselling, to spiritual direction. The common thread in the New Testament is that these are all ministries of the Spirit of Christ – the *Paraclete* – and their goal is to enable human beings to grow to maturity.

The second-century theologian Irenaeus, speaking of Jesus Christ as the glory of God, said, 'the glory of God is a human being fully alive'. That is the goal of *paraklesis*: for each person to help the other in the power of God's Spirit to become more fully alive.

The New Testament demonstrates a variety of pastoral guidance, not all of which would count as counselling in today's terms. But what each type is seeking to do is relate faith in Jesus Christ and the experience of God as Spirit to the messy business of living and working in this world. So St Paul writes about sexuality, marriage, incest, masters and slaves, employment, lack of church funds, care for children and so on. His is a world in which sin is real, in which pain is real, and in which people's lives get messed up and people hurt one another. But it is a world also in which relationships can be restored, and in which forgiveness, reconciliation, and a substantial measure of healing are possible. The goal is to move towards what Bishop Stephen Neill once called 'a Genuinely Human Existence', what St Paul calls 'growing to maturity in Christ', and what Irenaeus described as being 'fully alive'.

## Some history of pastoral care

In his classic survey of 'the cure of souls', psychotherapist and theologian John McNeill[2] illustrates the different emphases in the Church's pastoral care and counselling across the centuries. For example, he describes the age of the Church Fathers in the first few

2 J. T. McNeill, *A History of the Cure of Souls*, Harper & Row, 1951; cf. also G. R. Evans, ed., *A History of Pastoral Care*, Cassell, 2000.

centuries of the Church's life as concentrating on 'discipline and consolation'. The Celtic Church saw the rise of penitential discipline and the confessional. In the seventeenth century, Richard Baxter was known for his pastoral visiting and catechesis, and the Catholic tradition for the emphasis on sacramental ministry.

In the last hundred years or so, various factors have affected the Church's understanding of its role in relation to care and counselling. For example, the 1880s saw the growth of psychology as a science, and then the psychology of religion, made respectable by the Gifford Lectures of Harvard philosopher William James, and published as *The Varieties of Religious Experience* in 1902. Parts of the discipline of psychology then moved from the laboratory to the clinic via the work of pioneers such as Sigmund Freud and Carl Jung. Since World War Two, especially in the USA, the pastoral theology movement developed strongly in the work of writers such as Seward Hiltner, and this to some extent professionalized the work of pastoral counselling. From the 1960s, there has been a mushrooming of various 'schools' of counselling in the UK, eventually leading to professional accreditation through the Standing Conference for the Advancement of Counselling inaugurated in 1970. This became the British Association for Counselling in 1977, then changed its name to BACP to include psychotherapy in 2000. The trends of the last 30 years or so have often contributed to a lack of clarity about the Church's pastoral role, even a loss of identity for some clergy. A number of ordained people retrained as counsellors, believing that this was the only way to offer a fully professional counselling service. Others in the Church began to abandon pastoral caring and counselling as part of their ministry, thinking that this more properly belonged with professionally accredited practitioners.

## The conversation between theology and psychology

A number of models have developed for the relationship between Christian theology and the human sciences – part of the wider conversation that is still growing between theology and science in general. These models have affected the way the Church thinks of itself, and also the way the professional counselling world relates to religious and spiritual questions. Here are four such models.

## Four models of this relationship

### 1 Psychology against theology

This model is illustrated by some secular psychology that has no categories in which to understand spiritual experience. It has received recent publicity in Richard Dawkins's *The God Delusion*, in which he suggests that theology is a non-subject, and argues that religion (by which he means 'belief in God') is the by-product of some evolutionary mechanism. He shares the naturalistic explanations of religion expounded by Feuerbach, Marx and Freud. The same sort of argument about religions as a natural phenomenon is used by Daniel Dennett in *Breaking the Spell*.[3] The model also receives support from some Christians who see psychology as leading the faithful astray, and who retreat into a fundamentalist opposition to anything 'secular'.

### 2 Psychology of religion

As the title implies, the primary category in this model is psychology, though there is an openness to the reality of religious experience, or at least religiosity, within this growing discipline. The psychology of religion is seeking to understand the factors that contribute to religious experience from the perspective of the science of psychology. Pioneers such as William James and Edwin Starbuck in the late nineteenth century, and J. H. Leuba and Gordon Allport in the twentieth, have explored extensively the religious dimensions to human experience, and explored the meaning of such concepts as conversion, religious affiliation,

---

3 R. Dawkins, *The God Delusion*, Bantam, 2006; D. C. Dennett, *Breaking the Spell*, Penguin, 2006.

worship and so on. Coming himself initially from the discipline of biology, Alister Hardy set up the Religious Experience Research Unit in Oxford in 1969, and some of his successors, notably David Hay in his various writings, have documented and analysed hundreds of accounts of religious experiences of different sorts. Hay's most recent book, *Something There: The Biology of the Human Spirit*,[4] shows how, despite the decline of institutional religion, interest in spirituality is growing worldwide.

## 3 Complementary model

Many Christians who are scientists operate with a complementarity model in which human science and theology are both understood as offering insights into the truth of the human condition. There have been numerous conversations and symposia between clergy and doctors, theologians and psychologists. Some secular scientists see this as a valid model: Stephen Jay Gould argued that science and theology cannot be against each other, because they are 'non-overlapping magisteria' (NOMA). As he rather cryptically put it, 'Science gets the age of rocks, and religion the rock of ages; science studies how the heavens go, religion on how to go to heaven.' Understandably, Richard Dawkins does not like NOMA – but largely because he does not think theology is a subject at all. Typical of many scientists who are Christians is psychologist Malcolm Jeeves, who writes of the danger of opposing two or more accounts of the same events, thus generating unreal and unnecessary conflicts. He argues that science and theology are asking different sorts of questions; there are different levels of explanation, and different modes of interpretation. These can be complementary and not in opposition. Jeeves, for example, illustrates the different meanings psychologists and theologians give to the concept of 'guilt' – psychologists often refer to subjective guilty feelings, whereas theologians may mean objective moral guilt before God. He also describes the phenomenon of 'conversion' both as a psychological mechanism, and as the work of the Holy Spirit.

---

4 D. Hay, *Something There: The Biology of The Human Spirit*, Darton, Longman & Todd, 2006.

## 4 'Theological anthropology' model

In the 'conversation' between theology and psychology, theology is the large perspective within which the human sciences are understood to have their own proper place. This is a model of human life and relationships seen from the stance of the reality of God, and within which all other sciences have their appropriate level of discourse and interpretative mode. One example might be the wedding ring that John gives Janet. At the level of physics, this is a metal object with a certain density and weight. The chemist will tell us it is gold. But there is more to a wedding ring than physics and chemistry. The gold has a history – it was dug out of the ground, and refined, and made its way to the jeweller's shop where John bought it. It has an emotional significance – John gave it to Janet on a special day. It has a social significance – indicating to others that John and Janet are committed. It has a religious significance, given and received in the context of worship and prayer, as a sign of a covenant that John and Janet made to each other. It has a theological significance, symbolizing the endlessness of God's encircling love. Each level of meaning is important, but the 'higher' levels are related to, but not reducible to the 'lower' levels. Science tends to work from the 'bottom up'; theology tends to work from the 'top down' – with, in this example, the covenant relationship being a 'higher' level than the chemical make-up of the ring. All the sciences are held together, as it were, as horizontal co-ordinates by the intersecting vertical co-ordinate of the self-revelation of God in the incarnation of Jesus Christ. He is the Word, made flesh, right down to the level of our genes. This model says that all truth is God's truth, and that interdisciplinary conversation is all important in discovering more and more of that truth.

## Pastoral counselling

It is the third and fourth models that underlie the establishment of OCIC and similar organizations. Through the development of a theological understanding of what it is to be human, coupled with the insights of the human sciences as they are coming to be understood, the Church can deepen its own pastoral theology and thus its pastoral and healing ministry as well.

The Church can be more confident in its role of pastoral caring by drawing on and using insights from the human sciences, though not being controlled by them. It can see itself as a therapeutic community, drawing more on its rich heritage of insights into pastoral care, as well as celebrating the advances in the human sciences. The Church can use all these resources to strengthen our commitment to help one another become 'more fully alive'. Likewise, the professional counselling and psychotherapeutic worlds can benefit from the understandings from insights from Christian theology about what it is to be human, and particularly about some of the assumptions that undergird all counselling.

## Assumptions

All counselling takes place in a context in which certain assumptions are made – in particular about human nature, about what makes for a good and healthy life, about the processes by which people change. On each of these assumptions, Christian theology has some very specific insights to contribute. The following paragraphs will illustrate something of what I mean by counselling 'in a Christian context'.[5]

### Assumptions about human nature

My first set of assumptions concerns human nature. All counselling styles – whether relational or cognitive models of counselling, or the so-called 'moral' models such as Glasser's Reality Therapy that focus on personal responsibility – work with a view of what it is to be human. Christian theology has its own specific perspective.

---

5 See further F. Bridger and D. Atkinson, *Counselling in Context Developing a Theological Framework*, 2nd edn Darton, Longman & Todd, 1998, ch. 7.

Like all creatures, we are 'of the dust of the ground' in our evolutionary history. And yet we have that self-transcending capacity to stand back and think about ourselves and the meaning of our lives, which sets us apart from all other creatures. At one extreme there are reductionist scientists, who explain the wonder of humanity in terms of being only 'survival machines, robot vehicles, blindly programmed to preserve the selfish molecules known as genes'.[6] At the other end of the continuum, there are those who wish to divinize us, seemingly denying the material basis of our human nature. There is an ambiguity about our human condition, especially when we consider humanity's capacity both for great creativity, and for moral outrage. This is described rudely by Blaise Pascal: 'What sort of freak, then, is man? How novel, how monstrous, how chaotic, how paradoxical, how prodigious! Judge of all things, feeble earthworm, repository of truth, sink of doubt and error, glory and refuse of the universe!'[7]

This ambiguity is congruent with the Christian theology of humanity, as created in the divine image, and yet prone to sin. It does not sit easily with a thoroughgoing pessimism about human nature, such as we find in Thomas Hobbes's seventeenth- century *Leviathan*, which speaks of war of all against all, and life being nasty, brutish and short, or perhaps in Sigmund Freud's picture of a seething dustbin of instincts that need to be contained. It does not sit easily either with the optimism about human nature of which Jean-Jacques Rousseau wrote: 'Man is naturally good and – when he has had his dinner – is at peace with all nature and the friend of all his fellow creatures.' Or the optimism that American psychologist Carl Rogers shows in his belief that the innermost core of our nature is basically socialized, positive, forward-moving, constructive and trustworthy.

The New Testament offers neither an optimism nor a pessimism of our human nature, but an ambiguity, and an optimism of divine grace. St Paul put it like this:

---

6 Cf. R. Dawkins, *The Selfish Gene*, Oxford University Press, 1976.
7 B. Pascal, *Pensées*, Penguin, 1966.

I do not understand my own actions. For I do not do what I want, but I do the very thing I hate . . . I delight in the law of God in my inmost self, but I see in my members another law at war with the law of my mind, making me captive to the law of sin . . . Who will rescue me . . . ? Thanks be to God through Jesus Christ our Lord![8]

This ambiguity of our personhood is seen in various aspects of what it means to be a person. To borrow some headings from Scottish-born theologian and philosopher John Macquarrie,[9] we are:

## 1 Persons in the world

We live within the world of matter, in which molecules and genes are a significant part of our make-up, and yet that do not take away from us the freedom of moral choice. We live in an embodied world in which sexuality often drives our emotions and actions in directions of love or hate. We live in a natural environment that can be nourishing or polluting. This corresponds to a biblical affirmation of matter. It was of the material world that God said, 'This is good'. The material world was ennobled through the incarnation of the Son of God in the flesh, and the Christian hope is of the resurrection of the body, and the creation of a new heaven and new earth in which justice dwells.

## 2 Persons in relation

As the philosopher John Macmurray put it: 'The Self is constituted by its relation to the Other.'[10] In other words, human beings are essentially persons in relation to other persons. We are inescapably in a network of different relationships – to parents and siblings

---

8 Rom. 7.15–25.

9 J. Macquarrie, 'A Theology of Personal Being', in A. Peacocke and G. Gillet, eds, *Persons and Personality*, Blackwell, 1987.

10 J. Macmurray, *Persons in Relation*, Faber & Faber, 1961, p. 17.

and children, to colleagues and neighbours, and to society as a whole. This corresponds to a theological understanding that we are made in the image of God who is a Holy Trinity of Persons in relationships of love and communication and creativity. This essentially relational concept of the human person is a significant Christian insight.

### 3 Persons on the way

The divine image is both gift and task. The Scriptures refer to human beings as being made as God's image, and they also refer to our growing into his likeness. John Macquarrie speaks of Jesus Christ as the authentic 'human Being' and, in relation to him, he regards us as 'human Becomings'. The journey of faith is part of the meaning of spirituality, part of being incorporated into the Spirit of Christ, part of becoming more 'fully alive'.

Counselling in a Christian context is thus essentially counselling people who live in this material world; people who are in inescapable relation with others; people who are in process of becoming.

### Assumptions about values

My second set of assumptions concerns the nature of the 'good' life: what is it to be more 'fully alive'?

I recall asking a professional counsellor what the goal of her counselling work was. After a lot of thought she replied, 'I suppose it is to help people live with less pain.' Every counselling process will operate with some assumptions as to what makes people's lives better, what enables them to live with less pain or, as we might say, live more healthily. Here I draw on American theologian Don Browning's 'metaphors of ultimacy', which describe, he argues, the fundamental assumptions people make about their world, and which dictate the way they understand human life and behaviour. Sigmund Freud's metaphor of ultimacy,

Browning suggests, is 'mechanism' – the mechanism of biological instincts. By contrast, Carl Jung's metaphor of ultimacy is 'opposites' (extraversion and introversion, thinking and feeling, and so on) – the process of individuation in which opposing aspects of a human being are brought into a degree of harmony. For someone like the American psychologist Abraham Maslow, the metaphor of ultimacy seems to be the satisfaction of needs.

If we were to ask for a Christian metaphor of ultimacy, it would need to be a metaphor for God. Here, though, we need to be careful. I once sat in the gallery of the General Synod of the Church of England when the subject of debate was homosexuality. One person spoke of God as Creator and Judge, and spoke about sin and the need for repentance. Another of God as Saviour and Redeemer, about the possibilities of change, and the freedom of a new beginning. A third spoke about God as Lover, and the rich possibilities of the variety of our human createdness, of our differences being held together in the love of God. The important point is that in the debate the speakers did not *engage* with one another: they were working with different premises, and the fundamental metaphor for God with which they were working dictated the shape of the moral question and their pastoral response. Of course, God is Creator and Judge, Lawgiver and Saviour, Redeemer and Lover. He is enabler of community and giver of life. These point to a living personal foundation as the source of our values, a personal basis for morality, spirituality and healthy growth towards maturity, and the biblical dimension for holding this process together is the life of the Spirit of God within the Church. It is the Spirit that enables us to grow to maturity in Christ, and discover what St Paul calls 'the glorious liberty of the children of God'.


## Processes of change

My third set of assumptions concerns the processes to which we have just alluded – the ways in which people change. And here I offer two New Testament texts that have helped focus my thinking about the processes of counselling in a Christian context. The texts are from the Johannine writings. From the First Epistle of John: 'love casts our fear', and from the Gospel, 'the truth shall set you free'.

## Love casts out fear

It is a well-established feature of research into counselling that far more important than the psychological models used, or the techniques employed, is the quality of the relationship established between the counsellor and the client. When genuineness, non-possessive warmth and accurate empathy are present,[11] progress may be possible; when these are absent, it is less likely. All these are aspects, I believe, of love – the sort of love for which the New Testament uses the word 'agape'. It is a love not determined by the worth of the recipient, or by the satisfaction of the giver, but love that is given for the sake of the other. It is the vulnerable love seen in the self-giving of Christ.

When the relational models of counselling work in the secular world, they do so, I believe, because they are giving expression, albeit often unknowingly, to that central Christian insight that love casts out fear. In Christian pastoral care also, the quality of the relationships established is a vital part of the care being offered. Paediatrician, psychiatrist and sociologist Donald Winnicott wrote a book with the title *The Maturational Processes and the Facilitating Environment*.[12] An environment that facilitates growth and healing is one that gives appropriate expression to the love that casts out fear.

There are many fears affecting human beings, and fear is a word we cannot avoid when talking about vulnerable people. Abused people, for example, often speak of fear. The report, *Promoting a Safe Church*,[13] lists various effects of abuse: bouts of depression, anger

---

11 C. B. Truax and R. R. Carkhuff, *Toward Effective Counseling and Psychotherapy: Training and Practice*, Aldine, 1967.

12 D. Winnicott, *The Maturational Processes and the Facilitating Environment*, Hogarth Press, 1976.

13 House of Bishops, *Promoting a Safe Church*, Church House Publishing, 2006.

and hostility, inability to connect with feelings, behaving like a 'victim', low self-esteem, inability to form appropriate relationships, disturbed sleep, phobias and anxieties, self-harming, inappropriate guilt and shame, addictions, flashbacks of the abuse and so on.

Abused children may speak of bullying, of being threatened not to say anything; there is a deep fear of speaking out lest something terrible will happen.

We all know 'doormat people',[14] whose low self-esteem never allows them to lift their head up high and, at the other extreme, the perfectionists who are never satisfied because their standards are unattainable. Both can live in fear. We know the fatalists who have got beyond caring because they do not think anything they do will make any difference, and the dreamers who live in their own world of wish-fulfilment or nightmare because the real world is too difficult to face. Fear marks their lives too. Some people are so self-absorbed with their own needs and failures that they never appreciate how their story might impinge on others. Some are totally lacking in self-awareness and wonder why others find them so abrasive, boring and difficult to live with. Aspects of their lives are coloured by fear. How is fear cast out? Through love.

I was at a conference some years ago for those ministering in urban priority areas in South London. We were asked to bring a cardboard box to the conference, on which we then wrote down what it was that we thought got in the way of people we knew enjoying God's freedom in their lives. The boxes were then built into a wall right across the church. Interestingly, much of what was written concerned fear: fear of suffering, dying, old age or death; fear of police, of being mugged; fear of the authorities, of filling in forms; fear of noisy youth; fear of tomorrow. At the end of the conference the then Bishop of Woolwich, Peter Hall, took his wooden pastoral staff and knocked down the wall of boxes. 'Love casts our fear.' It was a vivid demonstration of the love of God breaking through the barrier of human fears.

---

14 Adapted from David Augsburger's exposition of Kierkegaard in *Pastoral Counseling Across Cultures*, Westminster Press, 1986, p. 338.

A facilitating environment, creating what the Revd David Gamble[15] called 'safer space' – whether that be family, community, church, professional therapeutic relationship or something else – can be the context in which fears can be faced, love received, and fears, to some extent at least, cast out.

We need to think of the pastoral care we offer in terms of providing a context in which fears can be appropriately faced, in which genuine love can be received, and a context in which healing, sustenance and reconciliation can be experienced.

When I was a curate in the 1970s, there was a period when my wife Sue was very ill. We had two young children at the time, cared for, for a while, by my parents in Kent, and then back with us in Birmingham. We needed a lot of support and care for some months, and the church where I was serving provided that. Someone even took us into their home for a while. Money seemed to arrive from nowhere to augment our stipend and help with travelling costs; people made us meals; two people in particular spent a lot of time looking after our two infants. In short, we felt loved. This was a very visible demonstration to us of the love of Christ in action. Here were God's people not only serving us, but proclaiming the gospel in deed as well as in word, as agents of God's purposes of love. Their service to us acted as a herald of the kingdom. And it was life-changing for us, and contributed significantly to our individual and family health.

## The truth that sets free

In the Fourth Gospel Jesus is depicted as affirming that there is a difference between truth and error. Human freedom is bound up with the personal freedom that a relationship with Jesus can give, but part of that freedom includes the belief system a person holds.

A rich young man came to Jesus[16] and asked what he must do to have eternal life. Jesus replied by quoting the Ten Commandments, all of which the young man said he had kept. 'What do I

15 Address to Methodist Conference 2009.
16 Matt. 19.16–22.

still lack?' he asked. Jesus said, 'If you wish to be perfect [that is, 'mature', 'fully developed'], go, sell your possessions, and give the money to the poor, and you will have treasure in heaven; then come, follow me.' When the young man heard this, we are told, he went away grieving for he had many possessions. Jesus faced him with the truth of his situation, which was being in bondage to his possessions. The truth pointed to a way of freedom, which sadly this young man did not take.

To take the example of abuse once again, part of living in the truth will be the recognition that if a person has been abused, that is an evil thing, and a great part of the appropriate response will be the quest for justice. Whatever we want to say about 'forgiveness', and I shall say more of that in the next chapter, we also need to hold on to the fact that God is a God of justice, and that the social dimension of neighbour love is to seek justice in all our human affairs.

Living justly, however, is sometimes complicated by the fact that many of us, much of the time (and maybe vulnerable people more than most), live in untruth. The psychologist Henry Ezriel wrote of 'the required relationship, the avoided relationship and the catastrophe'. By this he meant that we sometimes hold our-selves towards ourselves and towards others in 'required rela-tionships' in order to avoid facing other things. What those other things are we may not be able to say. We may not even realize we are avoiding them. All we do know is that if we were to turn to face them, it feels as if there would be a catastrophe. We imagine we would go over the cliff; the world would come to an end; a large hole would open in the universe and we would fall into it.

In the long process of pastoral counselling, which for some peo-ple may take years, the time may come in a relationship of pastoral caring when some of the unrealities of a person's life come to light and need to be faced, and then brought into the light of truth.

I referred in Chapter 1 to James Casson's booklet entitled *Dying: The Greatest Adventure of My Life*. What was significant in his perception that he had been healed, even through dying, was the release that came to him when he acknowledged the truth that he could do nothing about his situation. He had been worrying that he had not prayed enough, or not had the right attitude. Eventually the truth dawned, and he spoke of 'release'. That truth set him free.

Another example is of the disturbing and liberating experience a woman called Elizabeth had during therapy. She was a wartime baby, born to a single mother and to a family in which illegitimacy was an enormous social stigma. Grandmother had explained to her when she was a young girl why they had needed to move house: 'because of the shame, the shame!' So Elizabeth had grown up aware that she was the cause of the family's shame. She carried a burden of guilt, simply by being alive. It had all been her fault, she felt. She should never have been born. The blame was all hers. In the course of therapy years later, when she was in her forties, Elizabeth said all this to her therapist. His reply – in the context of a relationship that had been warmly built between them – was 'It is very hard to see why anyone could blame the baby.' This pulled the rug completely from under most of the assumptions on which Elizabeth had built her emotional life. It was initially very disturbing and unsettling, but ultimately, as the truth dawned, it was liberating and healing.

The psychologist Albert Ellis's work on reason and emotion in psychotherapy is an approach to the cognitive model of counselling that for some people is very liberating. He demonstrates that we human beings often live in untruth, which is reinforced by what we say to ourselves in our heads – our 'self-talk' – and this keeps us in anxiety and depression. A friend sent me a 'Christianized' version of some of Ellis's 'irrational ideas'[17] (which I have used before, but seem worth repeating here; Ellis himself was an atheist).

## The Ten Commandments of Self-Defeat

And the devil saith unto his angels: 'Wreak havoc on the earth. Create unhappiness everywhere. Sow fear, worry, anger and

---

17 F. Bridger and D. Atkinson, *Counselling in Context: Developing a Theological Framework*, HarperCollins, 1994 p. 199, referring to A. Ellis, *Reason and Emotion in Psychotherapy*, Lyle Stuart, 1973.

depression in Jerusalem, in Judea, and to the uttermost parts of the earth. For as I go, so send I you.' And one of these angels whose name was Blame, settled on the fertile valleys along the Ohio River. There he began to teach the ten commandments.

1. Thou shalt never make mistakes.
2. Thou shalt upset thyself when things go wrong.
3. Thou shalt blame thy neighbour as thyself.
4. Thou shalt neither love, nor forgive, nor accept thyself.
5. Thou shalt always expect things to be different from the way they are.
6. Thou shalt seek the love and approval of everyone for everything thou doest.
7. Thou shalt avoid facing life's difficulties, remembering that thou canst not change, because thou art trapped by thy past.
8. Thou shalt be preoccupied with whatever bothers thee.
9. Thou shalt wait passively for happiness to come unto thee.
10. Thou shalt be dependent mostly on others for thy happiness.

And as Blame taught the people of the valleys, they believed him. In great numbers they came, and heard, and believed, so that the earth was truly filled with fear, worry, and anger and depression.

The truth of God as it is made known in Jesus Christ in the pages of the New Testament puts a question mark against each one of these irrational ideas. Of course we shall make mistakes, we are sinful human beings, but God promises that forgiveness can be real. To live a life of blame is bound to trap us into the law of retaliation and revenge, which carries the crippling implication of stress and depression. The gospel is about reconciliation rather than retaliation. We are called to love our neighbours as we love ourselves, which implies that a proper place for self-love and self-forgiveness is an important part of our self-esteem. To find our worth through the approval of others is bound to lead to distress. The gospel is that our worth comes through God's gift to us: we are made in his image and we are precious to him. Our justification is through his grace, not through our achievements.

We are not in a fatalistic universe in which what we do does not matter. We are part of a story that God is telling about the world. The past can be put to rights – not changed, or forgotten, but lived with in a fresh way. Rumination can keep us trapped in negative thinking, and this leads to depression and anxiety. The Spirit of God can 'cleanse the thoughts of our hearts', and enable us to think on 'whatever is true, whatever is honourable, whatever is just, whatever is pure, whatever is pleasing, whatever is commendable . . . [whatever is] worthy of praise'. And that is liberating, and 'the God of peace will be with [us]'.[18] Finally, there can be the realization that, as at least two book titles have it, 'happiness is a choice'.

Cognitive therapies of various kinds, and the pastoral care that draws on them, can enable a person to live more in the truth, and so discover more freedom.

But it is painful and not easy. As T. S. Eliot put it, 'humankind cannot bear very much reality'.[19] Sometimes we need a lot of the loving that casts out our fears before we can face the truth that sets us free. But living in truth, and working for the justice that belongs with it, are aspects of the road to freedom.

For an abused person, for example, this involves the gentle and sometimes very long journey of coming to terms with what has happened, recovering memories, and finding appropriate and truthful ways of responding to them. It can take years.

For the abuser, healing comes through an acknowledgement of the truth of what has been done, and one's responsibility for it and for the hurt caused. This may go alongside living out the requirements of justice (in prison perhaps). It may take a person back into what might have been their own abusive childhood and help them face the things that have contributed to the person they are.

---

18 Phil. 4.8–9.

19 T. S. Eliot, from 'Burnt Norton', in *Collected Poems 1909–1962*, Faber & Faber, 1963.

## Pastoral counselling in a church context

Many churches are recovering the ministry of pastoral counselling as part of the ministry of the gospel. It is not the same as the mutual ministry of care, concern, listening and support that needs to be part of the regular ministry of each congregation. Pastoral counselling as such, whether in organizations such as OCIC, or adequately set up within a local church ministry staff, needs to be informed by the best insights of contemporary psychology, and to learn from the methods of accredited counsellors and psychotherapists. As in those professions, there needs to be adequate pastoral supervision of those offering counselling. There needs also to be a carefully understood professional pastoral counselling ethic. There is a danger of people who are not aware of what they are about doing more harm than good. Often the appropriate course for a pastoral minister is to refer a person in need to other agencies of professional counselling help. But, given proper safeguards and strict ethical boundaries, properly monitored and supervised, the Church *can* recover something of its rich heritage of pastoral care and counselling as part of its wider healing ministry. It can be part of the task of which St Paul prays in Acts 20.28: 'Keep watch over yourselves and over the whole flock, of which the Holy Spirit has made you overseers.' It can be part of what St Paul meant when he wrote to the Romans: 'I myself feel confident about you, my brothers and sisters, that you yourselves are full of goodness, filled with all knowledge, and able to instruct one another.' (Rom. 15.14); or, as the title of Jay Adams's book has it, 'competent to counsel' one another.

# 4

# Standing with the vulnerable: justice and forgiveness

One particular dimension to the Church's pastoral ministry that has received significant publicity in recent years is its work with the most vulnerable people in our society – the aged, the very young and survivors of abuse. Some of the publicity has rightly been very critical of the Church for its poor record in relation to child protection – a record that is thankfully gradually being put right. The Church's response to adults who are coming to terms with having been abused in childhood can either be healing or, regrettably, sometimes abusive once again. This chapter picks up some of the needs of abused people, whether survivors of child abuse or domestic abuse or victims of rape.

What is it that makes it so hard for some people who have been abused to go to church?[1] The answer is that often survivors of abuse don't want to talk about what happened to them, and most people in churches don't want to know – or live happily in the mindset of the curate who said of his large congregation, 'There is no one like that here.' So there are all the makings of a conspiracy of silence – one that is more comfortable to maintain than to address. The one place where survivors ought to find a

---

1 The first four paragraphs of this chapter are an adaptation of my article (David and Sue Atkinson), 'Abused and in Need of Apology', *Church Times*, November 2006. Cf. also *Time for Action: Sexual Abuse, the Churches and a New Dawn for Survivors*, CTBI, 2002, J. Chevous, *From Silence to Sanctuary*, SPCK, 2004, and S. Atkinson, *Breaking the Chains of Abuse*, Lion Hudson, 2006.

place of acceptance and healing is in the church, which is, ironically, the one place from which many feel excluded.

The statistics are familiar but still shocking: apparently about one in four girls and one in about nine boys are abused in childhood – sexually, physically or in other ways. Many survivors cope well and live normally. Some, however, although they present a 'normal' face to the world, may be badly suffering, often unable to say what the problem is. Depression, suicidal feelings, self-harming, inappropriate guilt, lack of trust in others, difficulties relating to those in authority, hostility, not wanting to be close to people, cutting off from reality – all of these may be symptoms of abuse. And the grim fact is that a significant number of people have been abused in the context of the Church by clergy, youth workers, and others in positions of responsibility – no wonder many survivors of abuse do not want to come to church. In a recent straw poll among a group of 60 abuse survivors, all of whom described themselves as committed Christians, only two go to church.

So what do survivors need from the Church? First, that it will try to understand how hard it is to belong. It ought to be obvious that the Church should be more compassionate and pastorally caring, and yet many survivors feel they cannot be part of it. The Lord's Prayer seems to require immediate forgiveness; words like 'Father' and 'sin' can trigger painful memories; the Peace can frighten those who do not want to be touched; anointing is difficult for people whose body boundaries have been violated; so is queuing for the altar with people behind you. One of the issues, of course, is power. All abuse is an abuse of power, which means that survivors often have a problem in responding to people in authority. Others are just scared – 'They wouldn't understand,' said Sophie, 'and I feel so ashamed.'

Survivors need someone to listen to them and, most important, someone to believe them – even if the story comes out incoherently. There is no quick fix for healing, and often professional counselling will help. Survivors need to be given time and space to recognize the effects of trauma on their inner world, and given support, as they work through their emotions, before they can forgive meaningfully. They need to make a start on dealing with their nightmares, 'flashbacks' (sudden intrusive memories), low self-esteem, phobias and debilitating fears. They do not need to be pressured into forgiving too quickly.

There are two key words – justice and forgiveness – that are central to the tasks of creating a safer and healing space within our churches, and the pastoral care of vulnerable people, among whom I include victims of rape and domestic abuse. These concepts of justice and forgiveness bring together some of the things we were exploring in the last chapter about love and truth. Both are important words loaded with Christian doctrine and pastoral implications.

Martin was a young person attacked at a church summer event by an older person. Obviously, he was very distressed. The vicar and many of the church officers said they knew the older person, and that Martin needed to forgive him and 'move on'. Martin's parents and others in the church said, 'No – this is child abuse, and we need to see justice done.' They wanted to inform the police and bring the perpetrator to justice. The vicar, along with others, strongly told them that it was not in the spirit of Christian forgiveness to inform the police. Hence the church community was split down the middle.

There is often, as in this example, a perceived tension between forgiveness, on the one hand, and the requirements of justice on the other. However, they belong together as both are expressions of the Christian calling to love our neighbours. Justice is the social and community expression of neighbour love. Forgiveness holds together much that is important about both love and truth.

## Justice

A report giving guidance to those with pastoral responsibility concerning matters of domestic abuse was published by the Church of England in 2006. It was called *Responding to Domestic Abuse*[2] and includes this sentence: 'It is of first importance for churches

---

2 *Archbishops' Council, Responding to Domestic Abuse*, Church House Publishing, 2006.

to offer sympathy and support to survivors of abuse and not to obstruct the provision of protection and the pursuit of justice.'

One of the criticisms of the Catholic bishops in Ireland who were castigated in the 2009 Dublin report about child abuse was that in their concern to safeguard the well-being of the Church as an institution, they did not take seriously enough the requirements of justice for the victims of abuse, whether child or adult.

The Code of Ethics for the British Association of Social Workers refers to social justice in terms of fairness of access to resources, equal treatment, reducing disadvantage and exclusion.

But what is justice? In many 'secular' professions the word 'justice' is used to mean exclusively or predominantly 'contractual justice', 'fairness' or, when speaking of justice in punishment, 'retributive justice'. This is the way of expressing the concept developed by American philosopher John Rawls in his now classic book, *A Theory of Justice*[3] (first published in 1971). He worked with the idea of an 'ideal just nation state'.

In 2009 Amartya Sen, winner of the Nobel Prize in Economics, published *The Idea of Justice*,[4] in which he criticizes Rawls and develops instead a concept of justice that asks: 'What is the just thing to do?' This refers not to an ideal world, but to the real comparative choices that have to be made in this world – judgements that tell us whether we are moving towards or away from realizing justice. His goal is to reduce injustice now, rather than try to create an ideal perfect justice sometime in the future. Both force on us the question: 'Is there a Christian idea of justice and, if so, what is it?'

## A Christian concept of justice

The biblical notion of the justice of God takes us into a different dimension. God is proclaimed as the one who 'executes justice' (Deut. 10.17–18). The psalmist's prayer for the king links

---

3 J. Rawls, *A Theory of Justice*, repr. Harvard University Press, 2005.
4 A. Sen, *The Idea of Justice*, Allen Lane, 2009.

together the creative power of God with God's concern for the plight of the marginalized:

> Give the king your justice, O God, and your righteousness to a king's son. May he judge your people with righteousness, and your poor with justice. May the mountains yield prosperity for the people, and the hills, in righteousness. May he defend the cause of the poor of the people, give deliverance to the needy, and crush the oppressor. (Ps. 72.1–4)

Isaiah looks forward to the time when God's coming King will execute justice:

> He shall not judge by what his eyes see, or decide by what his ears hear; but with righteousness he shall judge the poor, and decide with equity for the meek of the earth. (Isa. 11.3–4)

In the book of Proverbs, as elsewhere, there is special concern for the plight of the poor: 'Those who mock the poor insult their Maker' (Prov. 17.5).

Pope John Paul II wrote an Apostolic Letter in the year 2000 in which he speaks of the provision of the jubilee in Leviticus 25. He wrote, 'Justice, according to the law of Israel, consisted above all in the protection of the weak.' Divine justice merges into love and grace. God's justice becomes redemptive. Second Isaiah even speaks of 'a righteous God and a Saviour' (Isa. 45.21).

As we saw in Chapter 1, one of the remarkable aspects of Jesus' ministry is that he often reached out across the divide to those who were vulnerable, marginalized, and even outcast. He touched the leper, the dead body, those who were ritually unclean. These were vivid examples of his bringing life to the vulnerable – for example, vulnerable women and children. Face to face with vulnerable people, Jesus reached out across the divide to bring life and hope. Nowhere is this clearer than in his treatment of children:

> He called a child, whom he put among them, and said, 'Truly I tell you, unless you change and become like children, you will

never enter the kingdom of heaven . . . If any of you put a stumbling-block before one of these little ones who believe in me, it would be better for you if a great millstone were fastened around your neck and you were drowned in the depth of the sea. Woe to the world because of stumbling-blocks!' (Matt. 18.2–3, 6–7)

Jeffrie G. Murphy, an American professor of law and philosophy, wrote a book with the expressive title of *Getting Even: Forgiveness and Its Limits*. It argued that Christian compassion and forgiveness, important as they are, must not get in the way of a proper Christian quest for justice in human affairs. He would have been on the side of those church people who believed that Martin's case (see page 59) should have been referred to the police.

Justice, for Jesus, is closely related to *compassion* on the one hand and *judgement* on the other. Because of the grace of God in Christ, St Paul urges the church in Corinth to care especially for its most vulnerable members. In the coming new heaven and new earth, we learn that 'justice dwells', and the New Testament writers use this to spur their readers on to live holy lives in this world. Where does that take us? Human righteousness and justice should correspond with, and be transformed by, divine justice. God's justice transforms our human concepts of justice, and extends them into compassion and redemption. Justice is the social and political expression of love for our neighbours, and that includes both victims and perpetrators.

The Swiss theologian Karl Barth summarizes this so well, drawing on a famous text from the prophet Amos:

The human righteousness required by God and established in obedience, the righteousness which according to Amos 5.24 should pour down as a mighty stream – has necessarily the character of a vindication of right in favour of the threatened innocent, the oppressed poor, widows, orphans and aliens. For this reason, in the relations and events in the life of his people, God always takes his stand unconditionally and passionately on this side and on this side alone: against the lofty and on behalf of the lowly; against those who already enjoy right and privilege, and on behalf of those who are denied and deprived of it.'[5]

## Shalom: *peace with justice*

'Human righteousness', as Barth called it, is closely related to that other great Hebrew word that we have already discussed – *shalom*.

As we have noted, although *shalom* is often translated as 'peace', it does in fact mean much more than the absence of conflict. It is the absence of disorder at all levels of life and relationships. In summary, it is the presence of everything that God gives for human well-being in all areas of life. It means well-being in the widest sense of the word. When the *shalom* of the Lord is present, there are good relationships between nations and between neighbours. *Shalom* is about enjoying right relationships with God, with neighbour, within oneself, with one's environment. There is no *shalom* without justice, but *shalom* goes beyond contractual justice – in fact, it illustrates that justice, love, compassion, redemption and wholeness of life are all part of the same package. Frequently the Bible brackets peace and justice together, and the psalmist holds out the vision of the day that is coming, when God's salvation is at hand for those who fear him: steadfast love and faithfulness will meet, justice and peace will embrace (Ps. 85.10).

We need to hear Karl Barth's call for justice in the sense of God's stand on behalf of the most vulnerable. We need to learn that God's justice is redemptive and merges into compassion and neighbour love. We must be open to all the dimensions of *shalom*, as well-being at all levels of life and relationship. And we need to realize that divine justice transforms human justice into something richer and fuller than mere civic fair dealing and human rights.

One sad story of injustice in a church context concerns a woman called Cheryl, who was married for some years to Tom, a Free

---

5 K. Barth, *Church Dogmatics*, 13 vols, T & T Clark, 1936–6.

Church minister. There were times when Tom was physically abusive to both Cheryl and the children. Cheryl divorced him a few years ago, when it came to light that – so his children alleged – he had sexually abused both his son and his daughter when they were younger. Tom denied the allegations, threatening Cheryl not to say anything to anyone, and being physically abusive to her. When the case came to court, the judgement was that there was insufficient evidence to convict Tom and he was cleared. Cheryl received very little support from her church, or even from Tom's superiors, who said she was a 'troublemaker'. She still feels that a great injustice has been done to her children. The injustice seems compounded by the fact that Tom's church has allowed him to continue in ministry, not least ministry with children and young people. It is harder still that Tom has taken out an injunction preventing Cheryl from speaking of her 'side' of the story to anyone – something she has struggled with in her decision to speak about it with a trusted friend. It is hard not to conclude that the Church has colluded with injustice in this sad case.

God's justice means that the Church needs to stand with the vulnerable. We stand with the child whom Jesus sets in our midst. We stand with the vulnerable older person whom others marginalize. We need to seek their full welfare at all levels of life for them. It also means that we take seriously the judgement of the millstone for those who abuse the vulnerable. Justice does not mean softness – it means the harshest of judgements against those who hurt the weak.

A person I know was talking with a group of other survivors of abuse, and saying that, as a Christian, what one wanted for the perpetrators was God's best for them. Then she added that this might, of course, 'include a spell in prison'. *Shalom* does not override justice; it is peace and well-being with justice.

But justice does not always have to be retributive. It does not always involve the police, although there are legal requirements that in some situations of abuse of those aged under 16, the police must be informed. Some who have been abused do not want to go to the police, even though they may be obliged to if a crime has been committed – but they *do* want justice. This category includes children who would have to go through the trauma of a court appearance, which for many would feel abusive all over again. Some parents of abused children do not want to put a child through that (even though criminal actions must be reported), but they do want justice. So how can the Church respond to their needs? Many simply want to be heard, believed and supported, and for the painful journey of coping with recovered memories, triggers that cause flashbacks and all the side effects of trauma, to be one that they can walk with supportive Christian friends. Justice does not always need police involvement – but justice ought to be very much what the Church is seeking to work for and provide.

It is tragic when the Church fails in this. There are too many examples of it not listening to abused children or young people, who might then grow into adults so angry with its treatment of them that they then do go to the police, and sometimes want compensation. They abandon the Church because it is all too painful to cope with rejection, when they had hoped for compassion and support. In one case I know, the Church authorities continue not to listen to an adult, and the abused child inside him, and emotional healing has become impossible.

## Forgiveness

The second central Christian word I wish to explore is forgiveness. In his 1959 book entitled *A Genuinely Human Existence*,[6] Bishop Stephen Neill referred to what he called the 'three great enemies of human life: fear, frustration and resentment', and when speaking of resentment, he said that when he picks up technical books in psychology there is one word he looks for in the index and rarely finds – and that word is 'forgiveness'. Fifty years on, that is not true today. There has been a burgeoning psychological interest in forgiveness, and there is significant research carried out on the therapeutic value of it.

The danger today is that the word 'forgiveness' has become trivialized. All too often when a Christian pastor, in particular,

---

6 S. Neill, *A Genuinely Human Existence*, Constable, 1959.

has suffered some injustice, the media ask whether he is going to forgive his abusers. Some Christians feel under pressure, out of loyalty to their faith, to say that they forgive – and of course there are some wonderful stories of forgiveness that have been truthful, honest and liberating: from the father of the murdered girl at Enniskillen; from the mother of the murdered teenager in south London.

But for neither of these was forgiveness a cheap and trivial word. When asked what it meant for her to forgive the murderers of her son, this mother said she needed to do it 'every day'. 'Forgive and forget' is too cheap. Forgiveness in the sense of 'there, there, it doesn't matter' simply trivializes a great, but very difficult, Christian concept.

Once again, the example of the experience of abuse, and of survivors of abuse, illustrates the points clearly. It is all too often a devastatingly trivial use of the concept of forgiveness that is forced (not too strong a word) on survivors of abuse. On many occasions when Christian people have found the courage to tell their pastor or priest about past abuse they have suffered, a very frequent response is to be told that there is an obligation on them to forgive the perpetrators: 'If you do not forgive, God will not forgive you.' When such simplistic teaching is coupled with liturgies that often underline the significance of forgiveness, it makes it very hard for many Christian survivors of abuse to feel comfortable in church.

Forgiveness obviously is of very great importance, but in situations of personal abuse, what the Church says and does about forgiveness has to be held in tension with what the Church says and does about justice. Compassion for the victims requires that perpetrators are held to account for their sins. It is part of seeking the best for all involved.

## The meaning of forgiveness

So what does forgiveness mean? What does it mean for an abused child to learn to forgive his or her perpetrators? What does it mean for a bullied and bruised wife to learn to forgive her drunken husband? What does it mean for society to forgive a convicted sex offender?

To return to Stephen Neill's word, 'resentment', forgiveness is a process whereby I can learn to move away from the law of resentment and retaliation, and find a way in which the relationship – despite the injustice and the hurt – can move on creatively.

Essentially, forgiveness is about acknowledging that there is something wrong, but seeking a way in which we can refuse to allow the wrong to stand for ever in the way of restoration. Forgiveness seeks to use what has been wrong to build creatively for the future. It is to let go of the law of retaliation – 'You owe, so you must pay' – and move beyond the feelings of anger and grieving that can lead to bitterness and resentment. Eventually it is to move beyond legalities altogether into the fresh air of grace. In fact, 'letting go' might be a better way of talking about this for the survivors of abuse. 'Forgiveness' is really a relational word, and requires repentance – someone to say sorry. But the harsh reality is that sometimes the perpetrator does not say sorry, or is no longer alive. The 'letting go', which is for the abused person the very first step in forgiveness, might be all that can be achieved – and that in itself is hugely healing and re-creative. So we must not be trapped into thinking that forgiveness is a once and for all action. It is a process that takes time – as the Linns put it in the title of their powerful book, *Don't Forgive Too Soon*.[7]

Forgiveness begins with and includes acts of the will, but is a process, often repeated over time, which for some people can take years. It crucially includes 'letting go' of resentments and bitterness. But it cannot happen all at once. Of course, the mother of a murdered child cannot instantly forgive; there is anger and grief to work through. But she can grow to the point where the desire to let go of crippling resentment can give way to a process of actually letting go. It is helpful to distinguish between forgiveness given and forgiveness received.

---

7 D. Linn, S. Fabricant Linn and M. Linn, *Don't Forgive Too Soon: Extending the Two Hands that Heal*, Paulist Press, 1997.

Forgiveness reminds us of our human accountability. It reminds us that the perpetrators are accountable: they have done wrong, and wrong must not be minimized or trivialized. Wrong deserves punishment. But the victims are also accountable beings, with choices to make. However much the abuse has diminished a victim's quality of life, that does not mean that we cannot take steps to improve the future. We can make choices: we can ask for help.

In the last chapter we referred to the ambiguity of our human condition, showing how all of us have aspects of our lives that are both good and bad. We are wonderfully made in God's image, but also sinful, stupid and selfish. Forgiveness reminds us of this. We are not perfect, and will not be this side of heaven. There are good as well as bad things in ourselves and others. Forgiveness seeks to recognize the work of grace in ourselves and in other people: they make mistakes, they do evil things – just as we do. They have hurt us, sometimes in deep and lasting ways from which we may never fully recover. Forgiveness is about recognizing the wrong – not pretending that it did not happen, or that it did not hurt; not minimizing it, nor hiding it, but looking it full in the face while deciding that we will not remain stuck in a response of resentment and retaliation, however justified such an attitude may feel.

## The tears of God

Grace is not cheap; forgiveness is costly. The story of Hosea in the Old Testament illustrates the costliness of forgiveness, and the costliness of grace is seen most clearly in the cross of Christ, where – as American philosopher Nicholas Wolterstorff so memorably put it – 'the tears of God are the meaning of history'. The tender heart of God is broken on the cross, expressing the costly lengths to which God, in his forgiving love, is prepared to go so that relationships might be restored.

But forgiveness can heal. It is a process that takes place over time. Jesus tells Peter that it sometimes needs to happen not just once, but up to seventy times seven. The past cannot be undone, but its wounds can be healed, and there is no need for all our sins to accumulate against us for ever. By walking away from the burdensome law of retaliation, 'You owe, so you must pay', we can walk over time into the fresh air of grace.

Forgiveness is not easy, and is rarely instant. It is not the same as forgetting – for there are some things we will not be able to forget. But it is, over time, with God's grace, seeking the removal of the emotional power and pain of the past to set us again on the road to freedom. And it involves an action of the will.

Some of the things that we can do to help our clergy and Christian people become effective in pastoral care to abused people are, first, to recognize how very hard it is for some survivors of abuse to cope with church, and second, to teach more clearly about forgiveness – not as a cheap and trivial mantra, but as a deep, costly, but ultimately healing process of change.

One of the dangers of trivial forgiveness is that it can be used to suggest that abuse is ignored or minimized, but the other side of the coin of what we have said about forgiveness is that perpetrators need to be challenged to face justice. And for forgiveness fully to bring about a change in the relationship between abused and abuser, there must be repentance. Where there is no repentance, or can be no repentance because the abuser is no longer alive, there can still be the release and letting go of resentments and bitterness.

The sad thing is that even in the church, forgiveness has become trivialized to an easy grace: 'Forgive and forget.' But that is not in the Bible. One Christian mother tried to help her children to 'forgive and forget' an abusive father, and now deeply regrets trying to force an easy approach to forgiveness on them: 'I now realize that this was abusing them in a different way all over again.'

The fullness of forgiveness is a relational concept. There must be a giving and receiving of forgiveness for the relationship to be restored; there must be repentance and a change of heart, a willingness to ask for and accept forgiveness; and when that does happen there is joy in the presence of the angels. But repentance and receiving forgiveness can go hand in hand with police involvement and a prison sentence. Forgiveness does not remove the need for retributive justice – to some degree it depends on it. Full repentance includes remorse, restitution, reparation and resolution. This, too, can be a process that takes time.

## Social forgiveness?

But what of the social and political implications of forgiveness? Can societies show forgiveness? Some decades ago a member of the government got into trouble, and was forced to resign. He had committed what everyone understood as 'sin'. But after his resignation he quietly went about putting his life back together again, and did wonderful and quiet community service for some years. But whenever his name reappeared in the press, it was always coupled with a retelling of the story of his 'sins'. No mention of his change of heart; no mention of his good works. Again and again the press reminded us of his failure, his sin, his fall from grace. The law of retaliation was alive and well in the media. Would it not have been much healthier for our society – as well as more just to the person concerned – had the media been able to let go of the story of sin, and tell instead the story of grace? There could then have been a 'social forgiveness' of sorts.

And in international relations could there be a politics of forgiveness? There are styles of foreign affairs that seem to say, 'We have the weapons to be devastatingly cruel to you if you overstep the mark.' Instead, a politics of forgiveness would acknowledge the reality of evil, wrong and injustice, but seek to move beyond the law of bare retaliation and respond to wrong in a way that is creative of new possibilities. The Truth and Reconciliation Commission in South Africa is one example of practical politics built around the Christian concept of forgiveness.

## Healing for the Church?

So what of the Church as in institution? We have our share of wrong, of injustice, of evil. We have our share of abusers, and the history of the Church – especially with regard to child abuse, and in the misdemeanours of clergy, choir masters and youth workers – is sadly all too well known. What many survivors of abuse feel they need more than anything else is some recognition by the Church of what they have suffered and, for those who have been abused in a church setting, some note of regret and repentance. In 2004, the Anglican Church Synod in Adelaide passed this resolution. It is not by any means a blueprint for action elsewhere, but it illustrates something of the healing power of grace when an institution takes seriously the call to justice and to forgiveness:

> This Synod and we as members of it acknowledge with deep regret and repentance the past failings of the Church and its members. On behalf of the whole Church in this diocese, we apologise unreservedly to those who have been harmed by sexual abuse perpetrated by people holding positions of power and trust in the Church . . . We are ashamed to have acknowledged that we only took notice when the survivors of abuse became a threat to us. We apologise and ask forgiveness for the Church's failure . . . We commit the Church in this diocese to listen to survivors of abuse, to respond with compassion to all those who have been harmed . . .

Can we find a way in which this note of apology can also be heard here? In commending of the 2002 CTBI Report, *Time for Action*, the Archbishop of Canterbury, Rowan Williams, wrote:

> Few if any issues in recent years have so stained and compromised the credibility of various Church institutions and hierarchies as the record of ignorance and evasions over questions to do with the abuse of children and adults by Christian professionals, especially clergy. Honesty about this is painful, but essential for the Church's health and the Church's mission. This report is sometimes devastating reading, but it is timely, necessary and – if we are prepared to hear and act on some unwelcome truths – ultimately hopeful.

This is still timely.

## *Justice, forgiveness and the healing ministry of the Church*

There are several levels of involvement by the Church in the appropriate pastoral responses to vulnerable people. There is the level of policy-making and the drawing up of codes of practice for those who work for the Church. The Church of England, for example, now has a Safeguarding Officer in each diocese, and diocesan bishops are responsible for implementing a national policy for the protection of children, and for vulnerable adults. Training is offered for all who work with children, and the statutory requirements for police checking are carried out. There may still be a long way to go to root out all injustice, but significant steps have been taken in recent years.

However, pastoral ministry is not only about policies and their implementation. It may also involve providing a listening and supportive presence to someone who wishes to disclose something of his or her painful past. It may involve taking action to discipline any who work for the Church who have been involved in abusive behaviour. It could include a counselling ministry, if there are skilled people to offer it. It will hold, for vulnerable people, the tension between the demands of justice and the healing power of forgiveness, and try to see that both are enabled. The Church's pastoral ministry will be inspired by the compassion of Christ, and the quest for his *shalom*. Justice, forgiveness, compassion, redemption, *shalom* – all these are factors in the Church's pastoral ministry, and all meet together in the character of God who is faithful, steadfast love.

# 5

# Healing and the kingdom of God

Like a cut diamond, the Church's ministry of healing has many facets. The light shines in different colours, depending on the way you look. We have explored some of those colours in previous chapters, concentrating particularly on questions of emotional and mental health in Chapter 3, and on the needs of vulnerable people in Chapter 4. In this chapter I want to look at some of the other colours, in particular the relation of disease and suffering to sin, the question of miracles, and to conclude with a discussion of the sacramental ministry of the Church. But to do so, we need to stand back for a while, and take our bearings once again from the biblical story within which the Church's ministry is set. It is the story of salvation, the story of God's kingdom. That is a story we need to find fresh ways of telling in the context of our present culture and contemporary needs.

The philosopher Mary Midgley wrote in her book, *The Myths We Live By*,[1] about the imaginative patterns and networks of symbols that suggest particular ways of interpreting the world. She refers to such myths as the social-contract image of citizens as autonomous individuals, or the idea of progress, or the myth of omnicompetent science. The Christian gospel is of a different 'myth' (in Midgley's sense). It is a pattern and network of symbols in a particular story, and provides a better way – Christians would argue – of making sense of our world and enabling us to live creatively in it. It is a story about the creation's relationship with the Creator, about God's purposes for the world and his putting to rights the things that are wrong, about the coming

---

1 M. Midgley, *The Myths We Live By*, Routledge, 2004.

of his kingdom of justice, righteousness and peace. It is a story that holds out to humanity the hope of a future, and a grace to live creatively in the present. This is the story that is retold every time the gospel is preached, or the Holy Communion is celebrated. This is the story that makes sense of our individual human stories of joy and sorrow, sickness and health. This is the story within which the Church's pastoral ministry finds its meaning, and in which our understanding of health and healing belongs.

## The story of salvation

But first we will sketch the biblical story of salvation with reference to a few key people and events. We start with Abraham, and then look at the Exodus of the people of Israel at the time of Moses. We will draw a little from the times of the great prophets of the Old Testament. The Old Testament points us to the New, and the ministry of Jesus in the Gospels, and as interpreted by the writers of Epistles. We look forward to the fulfilment of God's kingdom in the vision of Revelation.

### Abraham and Moses

The story begins with God's call to Abraham to be the father of God's people, and the covenant relationship established between God and Abraham. Where the world had come under divine judgement, as depicted in the story of Adam and Eve's Fall from grace, God purposes to put things right, and begins to establish a new family with Abraham. The covenant refrain, 'I will be your God; you shall be my people', designated the close relationship between God and his people. It is a refrain that returns when God makes a covenant with the whole nation many years afterwards at the time of Moses. This is the time of Exodus, that pivotal event in the history of the people of God, when God, after bringing plagues of judgement on the Egyptian task-masters, rescued his covenant people from slavery in Egypt, and set them on course for the Promised Land. This is the meaning of 'salvation' in the Hebrew Bible: rescue and restoration of the covenant people. And it is in the context of that Exodus salvation that God speaks about healing:

> 'If you will listen carefully to the voice of the LORD your God, and do what is right in his sight, and give heed to his commandments and keep all his statutes, I will not bring upon you any of the diseases that I brought upon the Egyptians; for I am the LORD who heals you.' (Exod. 15.26)

As the leading New Testament scholar, N. T. Wright, puts it, 'Israel's covenantal vocation caused her to think of herself as the creator's true humanity.'[2] In other words, God is establishing a new humanity, focused in the covenant people of Israel, through whom he is putting to right all that has gone wrong in the world, depicted in the sin of Adam. The covenant is God's answer to the evil of the world. The Lord the healer is concerned not only with individual health, but with the health of the whole community – indeed, with the well-being of all creation. It is through God's covenant people that the whole of creation is to be healed, and all people become more fully human, more 'fully alive'.

The psalmist catches something of this blessing:

> Bless the LORD, O my soul . . . and do not forget all his benefits – who forgives all your iniquity, who heals all your diseases, who redeems your life from the Pit, who crowns you with steadfast love and mercy, who satisfies you with good as long as you live so that your youth is renewed like the eagle's. The LORD works vindication and justice for all who are oppressed . . . The LORD has established his throne in the heavens, and his kingdom rules over all. (Ps. 103.2–6, 19)

---

2 N. T. Wright, *The New Testament and the People of God*, SPCK, 1992, pp. 262f.

## Prophets

This story of salvation is told by the prophets of the Hebrew Bible, as in their different ways they call God's people back to their covenant obligations, and also hold out the hope that God has not abandoned the world, but is making things new. By this time, Israel had a king, whose ministry was intended to reflect something of the kingly rule of God. According to the prophets, Israel's God will fulfil the covenant promise; there will be a new world order. In the language of the prophets, there will be a king sent from God who will come and rule in righteousness.

> For a child has been born for us, a son given to us; authority rests upon his shoulders; and he is named Wonderful Counsellor, Mighty God, Everlasting Father, Prince of Peace [*shalom*]. His authority shall grow continually, and there shall be endless peace for the throne of David and his kingdom. He will establish and uphold it with justice and with righteousness from this time onwards and for evermore. The zeal of the LORD of hosts will do this. (Isa. 9.6–7)

This is the language of *shalom*, peace, well-being, health.

Even after the kingdom of Israel had come to an end, and God's people continued as the kingdom of Judah; even after the time when God's people had been taken into exile, God's prophets carried on with their message of hope, restoration and healing: 'I have seen their [wicked] ways, but I will heal them; I will lead them and repay them with comfort . . . Peace, peace, to the far and the near, says the LORD; and I will heal them' (Isa. 57.18–19).

The coming King is also depicted in the Second part of Isaiah as God's Suffering Servant, the one who brings healing to the people through his own suffering and death:

> Surely he has borne our infirmities and carried our diseases; yet we accounted him stricken, struck down by God, and afflicted. But he was wounded for our transgressions, crushed

for our iniquities; upon him was the punishment that made us whole, and by his bruises we are healed. (Isa. 53.4–5)

God's coming King (and his Servant) is also described (in the third part of Isaiah) as a Conqueror who will be anointed with God's spirit, and bring good news of healing and deliverance:

The spirit of the LORD GOD is upon me, because the LORD has anointed me; he has sent me to bring good news to the oppressed, to bind up the broken-hearted, to proclaim liberty to the captives, and release to the prisoners; to proclaim the year of the LORD's favour, and the day of vengeance of our God; to comfort all who mourn; to provide for those who mourn in Zion – to give them a garland instead of ashes, the oil of gladness instead of mourning, the mantle of praise instead of a faint spirit. They will be called oaks of righteousness, the planting of the LORD, to display his glory. They shall build up the ancient ruins, they shall raise up the former devastations; they shall repair the ruined cities, the devastations of many generations. Strangers shall stand and feed your flocks, foreigners shall till your land and dress your vines; but you shall be called priests of the LORD, you shall be named ministers of our God. (Isa. 61.1–6a)

Here personal, community and ecological health are all part of the picture. The context is of salvation (Isa. 60.18; 61.10), and of health. The two concepts are beginning to come together.

## The New Testament

The story of salvation comes to its fulfilment in the New Testament, and in the life, death and resurrection of Jesus. The prophecies of God's coming King are applied by the Gospel writers to Jesus. He is God's King who takes Isaiah's words to describe his own ministry. He is Prince of *shalom* (cf. Isa. 9.6). He is the one through whom God's covenant promises to Israel will come to their fulfilment, and his message is that God's kingdom has now dawned:

> Jesus came to Galilee, proclaiming the good news of God, and saying, 'The time is fulfilled, and the kingdom of God has come near; repent, and believe in the good news.' (Mark 1.14–15)

The Synoptic Gospels portray Jesus' healing ministry as a sign of God's kingdom, but St Paul's later writings see Jesus in a more cosmic perspective. It is the first chapter of the Letter to the Colossians that most vividly links Jesus Christ both to the creation, and to the covenant of redemption seen in the sacrificial suffering on the cross, and his now exalted state as the risen Lord:

> He is the image of the invisible God, the firstborn of all creation; for in him all things in heaven and on earth were created, things visible and invisible . . . all things have been created through him and for him. He himself is before all things, and in him all things hold together. He is the head of the body, the church . . . in him all the fullness of God was pleased to dwell, and through him God was pleased to reconcile to himself all things, whether on earth or in heaven, by making peace through the blood of his cross. (Col. 1.15–20)

Remarkably, here St Paul argues that the risen and exalted Jesus is the agent of God in creation, and has become the one in whom all things now hold together. But even more: it is through the crucified and risen Lord Jesus that all things, all people, all creatures, all creation, are restored into God's purposes, are – so to say – healed. Here is a vision of the cosmic Christ, and also a vision of a new creation. What has been fractured through humanity's sin in our relationship with the created order can, in St Paul's vision, here be put right.

So supremely in Jesus, creation and covenant belong together. Jesus, the Suffering Servant, represents both God's people Israel, and through them the whole of humanity, so Jesus the risen and exalted Lord represents the people of God's new covenant – the Church – and is in himself what true humanity was meant to be. He is the Whole Person.

That is not to say that the Christian Church already fully demonstrates the humanity that Christ came to liberate. We are still in a world under judgement, infected by sin, in constant need of healing, but the promise of God's new people in God's new world comes with the breaking in of God's kingly rule into the world in the life, death and resurrection of Jesus Christ. The Church is called obediently to witness to the Lord, living by his grace shown especially in the word and sacraments, waiting and working – with pain and struggle, sometimes – for the time when that kingly rule comes in all its fullness in the kingdom of Christ's glory. And that waiting and struggling is true also of the whole created order.

### The suffering creation and hope

The story of salvation includes the theme of struggling hope, developed by St Paul in his letter to the Romans. At the climax of his detailed argument in chapter 8, he writes:

> I consider that the sufferings of this present time are not worth comparing with the glory about to be revealed to us. For the creation waits with eager longing for the revealing of the children of God; for the creation was subjected to futility, not of its own will but by the will of the one who subjected it, in hope that the creation itself will be set free from its bondage to decay and will obtain the freedom of the glory of the children of God. We know that the whole creation has been groaning in labour pains until now; and not only the creation, but we ourselves, who have the first fruits of the Spirit, groan inwardly while we wait for adoption, the redemption of our bodies. For in hope we were saved. Now hope that is seen is not hope. For who hopes for what is seen? But if we hope for what we do not see, we wait for it with patience. (Rom. 8.18–25)

The first thing we notice about this paragraph is that in Paul's view, creation is 'waiting', 'subjected to futility', and 'groaning', and the sufferings of the present time are like the 'labour pains' of someone waiting for a new birth. In other words, in God's purposes, the whole of creation is expectant in its struggles and sufferings that a new freedom will be obtained. And then, second, the redemption of creation is linked to the redemption ('revealing', 'adoption', 'glory') of the children of God.

To bring these different aspects of Paul's thought together, in Jesus, the crucified, risen and exalted Lord, God has acted to redeem the world – and that means not simply humanity, but the whole created order. Speaking of the kingdom of God, glimpsed and promised in Jesus, the moral theologian Oliver O'Donovan wrote, 'In the resurrection of Christ, creation is restored and the kingdom of God dawns.'[3] And, as we have already seen, Hans Küng put it this way: 'God's kingdom is creation healed.'[4]

## The kingdom fulfilled

The vision towards which the biblical story points us is depicted in several ways in the New Testament. The Second Letter of Peter speaks of 'new heavens and a new earth, where righteousness is at home' (2 Pet. 3.13). The book of Revelation uses the same image, but in the context of the fulfilment of the covenant promise from God's throne:

> And I heard a loud voice from the throne saying, 'See, the home of God is among mortals. He will dwell with them; they will be his peoples, and God himself will be with them; he will wipe every tear from their eyes. Death will be no more; mourning and crying and pain will be no more, for the first things have passed away.' (Rev. 21.3–4)

---

3 O. M. T. O'Donovan, *Resurrection and Moral Order*, InterVarsity Press, 1988, p. 15.

4 H. Küng, *On Being a Christian*, Collins, 1977, p. 231.

And then, in a vision of God's kingdom, in which the water of life brings fruitfulness to the city, and in which nations too are healed, we read:

> Then the angel showed me the river of the water of life, bright as crystal, flowing from the throne of God and of the Lamb through the middle of the street of the city. On either side of the river is the tree of life with its twelve kinds of fruit, producing its fruit each month; and the leaves of the tree are for the healing of the nations. (Rev. 22.1–2)

## The Church's ministry of healing

The Church's ministry of healing is part of this great story of salvation. We are to be caught up into the healing ministry of Jesus, demonstrating the life of God's kingdom, as covenant partners with whom God dwells by his Spirit. We are to be anointed with that Spirit to live out the life of God's new world, looking for the day when God creates a new heaven and a new earth where righteousness is at home. Our prayer, every time we say the Lord's Prayer, is that God's kingdom will come on earth as it is in heaven. We look for the signs of its dawning,[5] and live and work and pray for its coming fulfilment. Our pastoral ministry is the working out of that prayer at many different levels, in medical and nursing care, in counselling for the emotionally needy, in standing with the vulnerable in their quest for justice and exploration of forgiveness, and in social and political contexts that make for community health.

---

5 'O God, who set before us the great hope that your Kingdom shall come on earth and taught us to pray for its coming: give us grace to discern the signs of its dawning and to work for the perfect day when the whole world shall reflect your glory, through Jesus Christ our Lord' (Percy Dearmer, in *Celebrating Common Prayer*, Mowbray, 1994), p. 98.

## Two frequent questions . . .

We are now in a position to examine in more detail two of the questions that arise in relation to the Church's ministry of healing – namely, the relation between disease, suffering and sin, and the question of miracles.

### Disease, suffering and sin

In Chapter 2 we emphasized that it is a mistake to argue that any specific suffering necessarily comes from a particular person's sins. Eliphaz does that in the story of Job, and gets it wrong. Jesus argues against this approach in his response to the disciples' question as to who sinned, 'this man or his parents', that he was born blind (John 9). But there is another dimension to this question that we need now to explore. There are examples in the Bible when it is clear that a person's physical ill health *can* be linked to specific sins. Miriam's leprosy in Numbers 12 seems to be directly linked to specific sin, as is that of Uzziah in 2 Chronicles 26.19. And the Bible states that cleansing from sin can alleviate depression (Ps. 77), or can even be linked to physical healing (the paralysed man in Mark 2.10). However, what is important in this context is not so much the specific sins that can result in a person suffering, or cause suffering to others, as the general fact of this being a fallen world in which our human condition is, as we argued, ambiguous. That ambiguity is part of the picture painted by the Yahwistic author of Genesis 2 and 3, where we find obedience to God giving way to rebellion, a sense of openness and delight giving way to shame, responsible living in the light of God and God's ways being clouded by guilt, and freedom in human choices becoming a sort of bondage. This is part of what is meant by sin – human life falling short of God's glory.[6] Its results, depicted in the story of Adam and Eve, are that blessing becomes a curse, sexual complementarity gives way to

---

6 Cf. Rom. 3.23.

subordination, work becomes toil, fellowship turns into banishment, and life is overcome by death.

This is the abnormal world into which God's word to Abraham comes as a promise of hope. This is the world that, in Jesus Christ, God has acted to redeem, and in whose resurrection, creation is restored and the life of God's kingdom has dawned.

So the Church now lives and ministers, as it were, between the Ages. The old Age of Adam is still there, and disease and death are still part of the story. Until God's kingdom comes in its fullness, creation, including our human bodies and minds, is still subject to decay. But in Christ's resurrection, the new Age has already dawned, and we can glimpse signs of it. Every time, through medical intervention, disease is held at bay, or through counselling someone is helped to live with less pain, these are signs of the kingdom. Every time someone is made more whole, or enabled to live a more holy life, through the ministry of prayer, that is the work of the kingdom. Whenever human communities are more ordered in the direction of God's justice, or God's *shalom*, they point to the kingdom.

There is no guarantee that sinful human beings will get it right. Despite our best efforts, there will still be disease, poverty, pollution, hunger and thirst. The vision of the kingdom does not rule out future catastrophes if humanity continues to misuse God's earth, and fails to live in God's ways. But as the psalmist said, even in death, God is renewing 'the face of the earth'[7], and the vision of the kingdom is ultimately of all things healed.

## Miracles of the kingdom

Miracles are sometimes described as rather clever events that break the laws of nature, and that are wholly inexplicable. In the Gospels, they are seen as signs of God's kingdom. There were numerous 'wonder-workers' around in Jesus' time, but what is different about Jesus is that his 'wonder-working' signs, often of

---

7 Ps. 104.30 (NIV).

healing, pointed to God, and were meant to lead to gratitude to God and to worship. The key thing about a miracle, then, is not its cleverness, but the fact that it is a breaking-in of the new Age of God's kingdom into this present one. The resurrection of Jesus is the supreme miracle in this sense. In the resurrection, creation is restored and the new Age dawns. In our definition of miracle, therefore, we need to be careful not to speak of 'breaking the laws of nature', but rather of an event that does not fit in with what we usually regard as 'natural'. As long ago as the fourth century, St Augustine argued that it is not that miracles are coun- ter to the laws of nature, but rather that they run counter to what we know of nature.[8] Our knowledge is limited, though gradually growing. There may be divine laws about the world of which we know nothing. Resurrection, for example, of which the resur- rection of Jesus is the forerunner, is, we believe, part of God's ordering of nature towards the new heaven and new earth.

In the biblical narrative, miracles tend to occur at specific times in history. They are reported at the time of the Exodus, with the miraculous release of Israelite slaves from Egypt. There are miracles again at the time of Elijah and Elisha in a context of conflict with paganism. They reappear at the time of Jesus and the early Church. Some Reformed theologians have argued that miracles ceased with the era of the apostles, but Pentecostal and charismatic experience in recent decades have increasingly challenged that view. It is true that there have been some Chris- tians who have tended to treat miracles as part of the normal life of the Church, and linked this to what has become an idolatry of health and prosperity. It has led to a manipulative style of ministry seeking the miraculous, and raising expectations among vulnerable people that cannot be fulfilled. It is never wise to try to manufacture the miraculous. We need to return to the biblical concept that miracles are signs of God's new order in our world, which cannot be programmed or manipulated, but to which we can be open with prayerful expectation and gratitude.

---

8 Quoted in C. Brown, *Miracles and the Critical Mind*, Eerdmans/ Paternoster, 1984, p. 8.

There are occasions when, in answer to prayer, unexpected things happen, even physical healing. There are occasions when a new insight into a person's emotional needs is given, transforming that person, and giving new insight into God and God's ways. There are times when, in answer to prayer, there is a sense of particular deliverance from what is felt to be an evil presence or force. These can all be signs of God's kingdom, and the breaking-in of the new order into our world. Some of them may be inexplicable according to our *present* knowledge; and others no doubt will remain unexplained for ever. Some events we may come to understand more fully as our knowledge grows. But we can call them 'miracles' if they point us to God and open us freshly to God's ways, and if they lead to lives of fuller gratitude and deeper worship.

## Humanity, the priest of creation

The biblical story of salvation, and the coming of God's kingdom, is the context in which we have set the Church's healing and pastoral ministry. One way of looking at our human role within God's creation is to speak of humanity as creation's priest.

Adam was given the task of 'guarding and keeping' God's garden, and humanity at work (and perhaps, especially for our purposes, humanity engaged in medical science) involves exploring ways of being good servants of the created order. In standing between the created world and the kingdom of God, interpreting the former in the light of the latter, humanity exercises the role of priest of creation. That priestly ministry is found in many forms. The theologian T. F. Torrance understands this priestly role particularly in relation to the healing of our split culture. Reflecting on the relation of science to theology, Torrance wrote:

It is more and more clear to me that, under the providence of God, owing to these changes in the very foundations of knowledge in which natural and theological science alike have been sharing, the damaging cultural splits between the sciences and the humanities and between both of these and theology, are in process of being overcome, that the destructive and divisive forces too long rampant in world-wide human life and thought are being undermined, and that a massive new synthesis will emerge in which man, humbled and awed by the mysterious intelligibility of the universe that reaches far beyond his powers, will learn to fulfill his destined role as the servant of divine love and the priest of creation.[9]

Another expression of that priestly ministry of humanity is seen in the healing and pastoral ministry of the Christian Church. Our service and our therapies, our prayers and our sacraments, are part of the role of the Church in acting as signs of God's kingdom, as priests of God's world.

## Healing and the Church's sacramental ministry

The Eucharist holds many of the above themes together. It tells again the story of salvation – a better 'myth to live by' (to paraphrase Mary Midgley). It unites creation and the covenant of redemption – the natural world and the world of people. The ordinary bread 'which earth has given', and ordinary wine, 'the fruit of the vine', gifts of God's creation, become for us the bread of life and the cup of salvation. The Eucharist holds out before us the vision of a sacred holy feast of sufficiency, in which angels, archangels and all the company of heaven share, reminding us of the holiness of God and the sanctity of God's world, and inviting us to delight in God's joy. It reminds us of God's law and our sin, our need for penitence and God's forgiveness, the centrality of love, and the prayer of hope that the day will come when 'justice and mercy shall be seen in all the earth'.

The Eucharist is centred on the self-giving love of God for the world and for us, the body and blood of Christ given for our

---

9 T. F. Torrance, *The Ground and Grammar of Theology*, University Press of Virginia, 1980, p. 14.

healing, and the healing of creation. Behind the Christian eucharistic liturgy lie the rituals of the Day of Atonement in which, through the gift of sacrifice, sin is forgiven, creation is restored and the covenant renewed.[10] In the Eucharist more clearly than anywhere else, heaven and earth come together in a foretaste of God's coming kingdom and the resurrection of all things into his love and his life. The liturgy ends with a commitment to a renewed allegiance, and the prayer that God send us out into the world in the power of the Spirit, to live and work to God's praise and glory.

## Creation healed

The vision of 'creation healed' commits us to the healing of divisions in our world, making poverty history, and working for an equitable distribution of the rich resources of God's earth. This healing, of course, reflects the whole breadth of God's kingdom: personal and social, political and environmental. The vision of a healed creation points us to the new heaven and the new earth, creation liberated by Christ, which is such a strong motivation for Christian concern for the health of our environment. It also includes a healthy social context for human flourishing. All this and more is part of the Christian story that the Eucharist is telling. And it is within this broader context of the healing of creation that the Church's ministry to individual people who are hurting is to find its place.

To say that 'God's kingdom is creation healed' is a reminder, as we have said before, that although there is substantial healing in the cross of Christ, the fullness of all the benefits of his passion do not come to us until God's kingdom is fully present. Just as there can be substantial freedom from some of our sins this side of heaven, though we will never be sinless in this life, so there can be substantial steps taken towards healing, even

---

10 Lev. 16; Heb. 9—10; cf. M. Barker, *The Great High Priest*, T & T Clark, 2003.

though it is only in the fullness of God's kingdom that we, with the rest of creation, are fully healed.

We conclude by returning to some features of pastoral ministry that can be illustrated by the pattern of the eucharistic liturgy. I am basing this on the form of *Common Worship* as used by the Church of England.

The liturgy begins with penitence, then it moves into the ministry of the word; we turn next to intercession, and this leads us into the sacrament of receiving Christ's body and blood to strengthen us to be sent out in the power of his Spirit. We will use these four themes as our headings for the rest of this chapter.

*Penitence*

Let us begin with penitence, confession and absolution. One of the features of the pastoral ministry of the early Church of the first few centuries was the development of a baptism discipline that included public confession of sin and penance. Later on, more formal 'penitentials' were written that laid down penances for certain sorts of sins. The biblical basis for this discipline were the New Testament examples of the baptisms of John, when the people 'were baptized by him in the river Jordan, confessing their sins' (Mark 1.5). 'Confess' is the Greek word *exomologeo*, which means 'speak out'. The public nature of confession seems implied in the experience of the particular church to which James was writing: 'Therefore confess your sins to one another, and pray for one another, so that you may be healed' (James 5.16). The belief underlying this was expressed by John as: 'If we say that we have no sin, we deceive ourselves, and the truth is not in us. If we confess our sins, he who is faithful and just will forgive us our sins and cleanse us from all unrighteousness' (1 John 1.8–9). With the rise in the power of the Church and its ministry, the practice of private confession to a priest gradually became part of the Church's life.

By the time of the Reformation in the sixteenth century, the emphasis was more on private confession rather than to a priest.

In a Church of England context, Richard Hooker, for example, writes that private confession to a priest is not essential, and he defends the General Confession in the liturgy as something that each penitent person can make their own in the quietness of their own hearts. In the Church today there is a variety of practice, though all would acknowledge the healing power of confession, and of hearing of God's forgiveness and absolution. Here is a more contemporary example.

Some years ago, a man came to speak to me about feeling depressed. He was married with two children. It emerged that he had been away from home on a business trip and fallen for a young woman, ending up in her bed. This was quite out of character for him, and left him with a sense of guilt. He had betrayed his wife, and let God down. He had been considering offering himself for the ordained ministry, but now felt this was out of the question.

After a period of talking things through, it became clear to him that his present feelings of depression were mostly to do with the guilt he felt before God. He eventually asked to make a confession. This was the hardest step he had to take – to *ask*. Rather like Peter in the Gospel, he avoided it for some time, and it took a great deal for him to set aside his pride and ask for God's help. He was used to fairly informal liturgy, so I simply gave him the service book we used each Sunday. He carefully and with considerable difficulty confessed to God what he felt was wrong and asked for forgiveness. I then read the prayer of absolution. And for him, at that time, that was enough. He relaxed, smiled, and was able to breathe fresh air again, and went home.

Forgiveness is not always so straightforward: sometimes it takes a great deal of time to find the will to forgive – as we saw earlier in the book, especially in relation to abuse. Many people's needs are more complicated than the man mentioned above, but for him this was a significant step forward in regaining his health. The Church's ministry of reconciliation through confession and the receiving of God's forgiveness is always available – for ourselves as much as for others. Sometimes this is best expressed through a much more formal setting than I used, with priestly absolution and the giving of a (private) penance, or goal for future life. The Church's ministry of healing invites us to be open to receiving and ministering this grace: ransomed, healed, restored, forgiven – who like me his praise should sing!

## Ministry of the word

The second part of the Eucharist is the ministry of the word in which the Scriptures are read and preached, and that too can be an aspect of healing. In Matthew's Gospel a description is given of the visit of Jesus to Capernaum, where a centurion asked Jesus to heal his servant who was paralysed. Jesus said he would visit the servant at home, but the centurion expressed himself unworthy of having Jesus under his roof, and said, 'only speak the word, and my servant will be healed' (Matt. 8.8). It was 'with a word' that Jesus cast out evil spirits (Matt. 8.16). St Paul describes his own ministry as of 'the word of truth, the power of God' (2 Cor. 6.7 AV). All Scripture, we are told in the Second Epistle to Timothy, 'is inspired' and profitable 'for teaching, for reproof, for correction, and for training in righteousness, so that everyone who belongs to God may be proficient [or complete], equipped for every good work' (2 Tim. 3.16–17).

It was pre-eminently at the time of the Continental Reformation in the sixteenth century that the ministry of the word became the primary resource in pastoral care. To give just one example, John Calvin, in his liturgy for the Visitation of the Sick, says that 'the office of a true and faithful minister is not only publicly to teach the people over whom he is ordained pastor, but as far as may be, to admonish, exhort, rebuke and console each one in particular'.[11]

The word of God is described by one biblical writer as 'living and active, sharper than any two-edged sword, piercing until it

---

11 Quoted in J. T. McNeill, *A History of the Cure of Souls*, Harper & Row, 1951, p. 197.

divides soul from spirit, joints from marrow; it is able to judge the thoughts and intentions of the heart' (Heb. 4.12). In fact, the word carries with it a sense of power; it is not just the imparting of information. If the churchwarden in a church came running down the aisle shouting 'Fire, Fire!' he would not simply be imparting information. He would be expecting and evoking and empowering a response. The word of God can powerfully cut through our pretences and the ways we live in untruth. It does not only talk about liberation, it can liberate. It does not only talk about joy, it can give joy.

Through narrative and poetry, through prophecy and vision, the Scriptures tell us about God and his ways, and that can bring healing. As a wise person said a long time ago: 'Do not be wise in your own eyes; fear the LORD, and turn away from evil. It will be a healing for your flesh and a refreshment for your body' (Prov. 3.7). Centuries before Helen Flanders Dunbar wrote her medical books about psychosomatic illness in the early twentieth century, the writer of Proverbs was telling us that a God-fearing attitude to life and an appropriate lifestyle based on God's word will have a healing effect on our bodies. Thus the Church's ministry of healing is rooted in God's life-giving word.

### Intercessory prayer

A third aspect of the Church's ministry in relation to healing is prayer.

It is, of course, always important to make time to wait for God and listen to him, especially in the rush and exhaustion of contemporary life. The psalms are full of encouragement concerning making space to listen. That space can be healing. Many people find a regular retreat a time of refreshment and healing. Every Sunday we pray for those who are unwell, those in hospital, those bereaved. And sometimes, also, it can be a very important part of someone's stepping towards wholeness for a very particular time to be set aside to pray with, and for, that person.

The Epistle of James illustrates the practice of the early Church. James 5.13 asks, 'Are any among you sick? They should call for the elders of the church and have them pray over them, anointing them with oil in the name of the Lord' (NLT).

Although there is little clear evidence for the anointing of the sick in the early Church, it is clear that it was used with penance when a person was dying. However, the Venerable Bede wrote in the eighth century that it had been the custom of the Church from apostolic times for presbyters to anoint the sick with consecrated oil and to pray for their healing. By the fourteenth century, the Catholic Church was speaking about seven sacraments, the anointing of the sick being among them.[12]

Some of the most poignant moments of my own ministry have been times when, after a period of counselling with someone, I have said, 'If you ever feel it right for us to set aside some time to pray, perhaps with one or two others, perhaps to anoint you with oil as a sign and encouragement in our prayers, please ask.' And when on occasion people have asked, and we have prayed, laying on our hands as a reminder of God's loving touch on our lives, and anointing with oil, these have been important moments of growth towards fuller health.

'I anoint you with oil in the name of the Lord Jesus Christ. May our heavenly Father make you whole in body and mind, and grant you the inward anointing of his Holy Spirit.' In this prayer we must remember two things. First, that the responsibility for asking rests with the ill person. This is not a ministry to be *imposed*; rather, we let it be known that it is available. Second, prayer is not about telling God what to do; it is about opening ourselves to God's will, his life, his love, his grace. And whether or not he meets us in the way we would choose, such an encounter in its broadest sense is always healing: 'My grace', he said to St Paul, 'is sufficient for you.'

---

12 R. P. McBrien, 'The Sacraments of Healing', in G. R. Evans, ed., *A History of Pastoral Care*, Cassell, 2000, pp. 407f.

## Special healing services

It is within these 'rules of prayer' that special healing services in church belong. Sometimes they are advertised in a church programme to suggest that God will do certain miracles at 6:30 p.m. on Sunday. I believe that we need to take great care not to suggest that prayer is about telling God what to do. I was present with some friends at a service in the Cape Town township of Khayelitsha. A friend was not well, and she was invited to come forward for prayer, and others of us were invited to share in laying on our hands. One of my colleagues felt unable to take part, because he believed that to do so would raise unrealistic expectations of instant healing, and would be a form of trying to manipulate God. Others of us felt that what we were doing was offering to God our concerns about our sick friend, and praying that God would meet her in grace in whatever way was best for her. She was not instantly healed, but she felt considerably strengthened in her spirit through the prayers that were offered.

## 'Gifts of healings'

The New Testament sometimes refers to specific *charismata* – spiritual gifts that help Christians exercise their ministry within the Church. They seem to have been unusual expressions of God's grace – some miraculous, some not miraculous. They are gifts of the Holy Spirit, given for the edification of the Church (1 Cor. 12). Among these are what are called 'gifts of healing' (1 Cor. 12.9, 28, 29). St Paul associates healing with the 'gift of faith' (in the first part of verse 9), and the implication may be that not everyone who needs healing may have the necessary gift of faith.[13] The gifts are given to the Church as a whole, and though sometimes one person may appear to have a particular gift, the emphasis in St Paul's writing is that they are corporate

---

13 A. C. Thiselton, *The First Epistle to the Corinthians*, Eerdmans/ Paternoster, 2000, commentary on 1 Corinthians 12.9.

rather than individual. It is not so much, therefore, that a person 'has a gift'. It is rather that the whole Church is gifted by the Holy Spirit for certain situations, as need arises and prayerful faith is exercised.

## Inner healing

As I was writing this, a Christian friend who had been ill for a long time telephoned unexpectedly to say that she had experienced considerable healing. The long story includes the fact that her mother had treated her very aggressively when she was young, for which my friend had long ago forgiven her, but her mother's actions had contributed to various physical and psychosomatic ailments in later life. Recently, someone from the church had called to see how things were and, rather unusually, had asked whether she could pray for her. A simple prayer was said, during which, unbidden and unexpectedly, my friend had a picture of Jesus come into her mind. Jesus placed himself between my friend and her mother in her mind's eye, and gently pushed my friend away from her mother, so that eventually there was a considerable distance between them, with Jesus between. The whole experience was one of tremendous release, with tears, of a childhood hurt and pain that had exercised its power over my friend for many years. This was not a formal setting for prayer; there was no expectation of a ministry of healing. My friend takes it as a gracious gift of the Lord. It is what many would call 'inner healing', or 'healing of the memories', and is a form of deep therapy of the Spirit.

## Deliverance ministry

One rather specialized form of intercessory prayer concerns those who feel themselves to be afflicted by evil forces of one sort or another. Very occasionally it may be appropriate to speak of someone being 'possessed' by evil, and there are procedures in most churches, under appropriate authority and in consultation with psychiatric and medical services, for a careful rite of exorcism. But that is very rare. Somewhat more common are those who feel oppressed by a force outside them, or who have experienced something strange about their environment – feeling cold, aware of a 'presence', or conscious of a compulsion to do something they would rather not do. In such cases prayer for deliverance may be appropriate. This is most helpfully undertaken by a group of praying friends, and needs to be quiet and unobtrusive, resting on the petition in the Lord's Prayer, 'Deliver us from evil'. One helpful introduction to this ministry is John Richards's book, *But Deliver Us From Evil*.[14]

## Holy Communion

The Eucharist comes to its climax in the ministry of the sacrament with the prayer of Thanksgiving, and the receiving of Holy Communion. Nowhere more clearly do the circle of my need and the circle of God's grace intersect than in the broken bread and poured-out wine of the Eucharist. Each communion can be a time when, with empty hands, we receive again the body and blood of Christ, his self-giving love, the tokens of his grace, and the strength to become a little more whole.

So the liturgy of the Eucharist brings together the ministry of forgiveness, of word, of prayer, of grace. It links the present to the past and to the future. It looks back to the death of Christ and the gift of his life for us. It looks forward to the coming kingdom of his glory when all shall be made whole, and creation will be healed. And in the present we commune with Christ, and in fellowship with one another, to receive the remission of our sins and all other benefits of his passion.

As Archbishop Michael Ramsey once put it, in a paragraph that begins with the Church here and now but broadens the vision to include the whole of creation:

---

14 J. Richards, *But Deliver Us From Evil*, Darton, Longman & Todd, 1974.

Nowhere more vividly than in the sacrament of the Eucharist do Christians find through Christ an openness to the past and to the present, to heaven and to the world. The sacrifice of Christ on Calvary is present in the here and now in its timeless potency, and the homely bread and wine of a contemporary meal are made the effectual signs of Christ's self-giving. The Christian community on earth is one with the saints in heaven. Blending past and present, earth and heaven, the Eucharist is a prophecy and a prayer for our coming to the vision of God and for the coming of God's reign in the world.[15]

That is a vision of wholeness, of good health – 'coming to the vision of God' and 'the coming of God's reign in the world'. God give us grace to keep on growing towards God's kingdom:

May we who share Christ's body live his risen life; we who drink his cup bring life to others; we whom the Spirit lights give light to the world. Keep us firm in the hope you have set before us, so we and all your children will be free, and the whole earth live to praise your name; through Christ our Lord.[16]

15 A. M. Ramsey, *God, Christ and the World,* SCM, 1969, p. 116.
16 From the Church of England, *Common Worship: Services and Prayers for the Church of England*, Church House Publishing, 2000, p. 182.

# Index

Hardy, A. 42
Hay, D. 42
healing services 93
health 4, 7, 96
Hick, J. 26
Hiltner, S. 19, 40
hope 79ff.
Hurding, R. 22

illness 5
inner healing 94
intercessory prayer 91f.
Irenaeus 39
Israel, M. 26, 32

James, W. 40
Jeeves, M. 42
Jesus' ministry of healing 11,
    14f., 77ff.,
Job, Book of 20, 26ff., 82
John, J. 15
John Paul II, Pope 61
justice 57ff., 59ff., 60, 62,
    63f., 72

kingdom of God 80f., 83f.
Kung, H. 10, 80

Lake, F. 22
Lewis, C. S. 27, 28, 31
Lightfoot, J. B. 8
Linn, D., S., & M. 67 nil
Lloyd Jones, M. 19
love 49ff.

Macmurrary, J. 46
Macquarrie, J. 46, 47

McAll, K. 23
McNeil, J. T. 39, 90
medicine 8, 13–14
Midgley, M. 73
ministry of the Word 90f.
miracle 83f.
Moltmann, J. 4
Monod, J. 27
Murphy, J. G. 62

Neill, Bishop S. 39, 65
nurture 20

O'Donovan, O. 80
Oxford Christian Institute
    for Counselling 36ff., 43,
    56

*paraklesis* 38
pastoral care 19f., 39ff.
pastoral counselling 43ff.,
    56ff.
penitence 88
Polkinghorne, J. 34
prayer 23
priest of creation 85
*Promoting a Safe Church*
    49
psychology 40ff.

Ramsey, Archbishop Michael
    95, 96
Rawls, J. 60
Reformation 18
Religious Experience Research
    Unit 42
resentment 65, 67